Erich Schneider-Wessling
Architekt BDA im Bauturm Köln

... und das nenne ich
REALE ARCHITEKTUR

... and that is what I call REAL ARCHITECTURE

Herausgegeben von ■ *Edited by* Octavianne Hornstein

INHALT ■ *CONTENTS*

04   REALE ARCHITEKTUR ■ *REAL ARCHITECTURE*

10   Ort ■ *Location*

12   Neue Stadtmitte, Kaarst ■ *New Civic Centre, Kaarst*

22   Klima ■ *Climate*

24   Deutsche Bundesstiftung Umwelt, Osnabrück ■ *Federal German Foundation for the Environment, Osnabrück*

30   Natur einschalten ■ *Restoring the natural environment*

32   Kommunikationszentrum der Bayer AG, Leverkusen ■ *Bayer AG Communication Centre, Leverkusen*

38   Individualität ■ *Individuality*

40   Wohnhaus in der Josephstraße, Köln ■ *House in Josephstrasse, Cologne*

44   Kommunikation ■ *Communication*

46   Wohnbebauung Spargelacker, Hannover ■ *Spargelacker Housing Development, Hanover*

54   Moderne Techniken ■ *Modern technology*

56   Büros und Montagehalle, Köln ■ *Offices and Assembly Hall, Cologne*

62   Angemessene Mittel ■ *Appropriate means*

64   Erweiterung des Bauturm, Köln ■ *Extension of Bauturm Offices, Cologne*

68   Lebenslauf ■ *Curriculum vitae*

69   Werkverzeichnis ■ *Showcase*

71   Mitarbeiter ■ *Staff*

72   Impressum ■ *Acknowledgements*

REALE ARCHITEKTUR ■ *REAL ARCHITECTURE*

Die Entwicklung des Menschen und der Umwelt führt durch bewußtes Handeln mit Prinzipien, die sich in der jeweiligen Zeit einstellen, zu immer neuen Ergebnissen der Baukultur.

Die klassische Moderne hat die Gleichheit der Individuen und das Recht auf angemessenen Wohnraum verfolgt. Die zweite Phase der Moderne, der Strukturalismus der 60er Jahre, greift die sozialen Defizite auf und befaßt sich mit den Kommunikationsbedürfnissen der Menschen. In der dritten Phase wird aus dem Bewußtsein heraus, daß der Fortschrittsglaube zur Zerstörung der Umwelt führt, ein ökologisches Handeln gefordert.

Meine Auffassung von Architektur fußt in der Haltung meiner Lehrer Frank Lloyd Wright und Richard Neutra; seine „Architectural Philosophy" war der „Biorealismus", die Wissenschaft vom Einfluß des Raums auf das biologische und psychische Wohlbefinden des Menschen. Die Beschäftigung mit den Beziehungen der Menschen untereinander hat uns in den 60er Jahren zu Themen des „Urbanen Wohnens" und der Raumstadtideen geführt; ich sprach damals scherzhaft vom „Soziorealismus".

Als mit der Ölkrise der 70er Jahre klar wurde, daß die fossilen Energien begrenzt sind und daß wir mit ihrer Ausbeutung die Existenz unserer Erde in Gefahr bringen, haben wir uns intensiv mit energieorientiertem Bauen befaßt. Ökologie ist das Gebot der Zeit.
Ist es die Zeit des Ökorealismus? Sind jetzt Bio- und Sozialfaktoren out?

Natürlich nicht, es sind dies keine Zeiterscheinungen, die mit „-ismen" bezeichnet werden, sondern andauernde Realitäten für das kommende Jahrtausend.

Wissen wird angereichert, das in der künftigen Architektur eine determinierende Rolle spielt; diese nenne ich die „Reale Architektur". Nicht eine zeitgebundene formale Mode ist meiner Meinung nach Architektur, sondern der gesellschaftliche Auftrag, mit möglichst viel Information über das Befinden von Menschen in Räumen in unterschiedlichen Klimazonen, über Situationen, die die Beziehungen der Menschen fördern, und über die Verträglichkeit von künstlichen – baulichen – Eingriffen in die Umwelt, Städte und Häuser herzustellen.

Seit Gründung des Aufbaustudiums „Reale Architektur" an der Akademie der Bildenden Künste in München haben wir über diese Inhalte nachgedacht und es haben sich sieben Schwerpunkte herausgestellt, die wir in der folgenden Kurzfassung beschreiben.

Ort:
Rücksicht und Neubestimmung der vorhandenen Bebauung oder Landschaft
Klima:
Abhängigkeit von der spezifischen Klimazone
Natur:
Wechselbeziehung von Natur, Mensch und Architektur
Technik:
Anwendung moderner Techniken
Mittel:
Erschließen angemessener ökonomischer Ressourcen
Kommunikation:
Architektonische Angebote für die Gemeinschaft
Individuum:
Physische und psychische Bedürfnisse des Menschen

Beziehungsdiagramm „REALE ARCHITEKTUR" ■ „REAL ARCHITECTURE" Diagram of relationships

Wir haben begriffen, daß beim Entwurf eines Hauses alle Erkenntnisse gleichzeitig, wenn auch nicht gleichgewichtet, zum Tragen kommen; dies soll die Beziehung der Schwerpunkte untereinander zum Ausdruck bringen: Dabei behandeln die Schwerpunkte den jeweilgen Wissensstand über Grundlagen und Anwendung bei der Planung.

Kürzlich haben wir nach 15 Jahren an der Akademie München in einem zweisemestrigen Seminar die Vollständigkeit und Aktualität der Schwerpunkte hinterfragt. Wir sind zu dem Ergebnis gekommen, daß nicht mehr so viel vom Bauen für Gemeinschaften gesprochen wird, dafür aber das Befinden des Individuums im Vordergrund steht. Moderne Techniken beherrschen die Architekturszene, wohingegen sich wenige Erkenntnisse über die Rolle der Natur in der geplanten Umwelt angesammelt haben. Gleichbedeutend ist der Einfluß des Ortes, obwohl ein neuer Trend der Vereinfachung mit monumentaler Haltung die Rücksicht auf landschaftliche und bauliche Bestimmungsfaktoren zu vernachlässigen scheint.

Das Bewußtsein für den Einsatz angemessener Mittel ist zwar gewachsen, aber die immer komplexer werdenden Bautechniken und unübersehbaren Vorschriftenberge versperren den Blick auf das Einfache. Als neuer Schwerpunkt erscheint am Horizont der Einfluß der Elektronik und der Mikrobiologie auf unser Leben, sowie die Auswirkungen der verschiedenen Migrationen. Die Auswirkungen der Elektronik in verschiedenen Bereichen der Architektur haben wir diskutiert und uns die Frage gestellt: Stehen wir vor einer Zeit der „Virtuellen Architektur"?

Die Einschaltung des Computers beim Entwurfsprozeß führt durch Einfachheit der Repetition und Schnelligkeit des Prozesses im Vergleich zu herkömmlichen Methoden zu weniger innovativen Ergebnissen, zu Simplifizierungen. Aber hier möchte ich vorsichtig sein, sind doch manche Computerfreaks genial bei der Anwendung des elektronischen Geräts. Da die Kinder mit dieser Technik aufwachsen, werden die nächsten Generationen vielleicht mit der gleichen Leichtigkeit die Maus einsetzen wie wir Stift und Skizzenblock.

Gegenwärtig stellt die virtuelle Welt einen aktuellen Diskussionsansatz dar, der einen Schwerpunkt im System der „Realen Architektur" bilden kann. In diesem Buch sind die Schwerpunkte der „Realen Architektur" beschrieben. Diesen sind Projekte zugeordnet, bei denen die Inhalte eine vorrangige Rolle spielen. Außerdem ist aufgezeigt, wo bei anderen Projekten der jeweilige Schwerpunkt vorkommt. Dadurch soll das ganzheitliche System der „Realen Architektur" beim Entwicklungsprozess der Entwürfe durch gebaute Ergebnisse demonstriert werden. Ein Anspruch auf Vollständigkeit verbietet sich schon deshalb, weil sich immer neue Erkenntnisse einstellen.

Viele Architekten beschäftigen sich mit ähnlichen Inhalten, ohne sich der Systematik der „Realen Architektur" zu bedienen. Auch wir gehen oft intuitiv vor, aber zur Überprüfung der Vollständigkeit führt uns der Beziehungskreis oft zu reicheren Ergebnissen, die häufig nicht den formalen Trends folgen. Auch wenn wir an der Gestaltfindung für vorgefundene Inhalte intensiv arbeiten, ist uns inhaltloses Design fremd.

Erich Schneider–Wessling

Human development and the development of our environment give rise to ever new phenomena in our building culture if we act consciously in accordance with the prevailing principles of our age.

The classical Modern Movement pursued the ideals of the equality of all men and the right to adequate living space. The second phase of modern architecture, which manifested itself in the Structuralism of the 60s, addressed the question of social shortcomings and was concerned with the communicational needs of man. In the third phase, our awareness that a blind belief in progress is leading to the destruction of our environment has resulted in calls for ecological action.

My own concept of architecture is based on the ideas of my mentors Frank Lloyd Wright and Richard Neutra. Neutra's architectural philosophy is to be found in "biorealism", the science that examines the influence of space on man's biological and emotional sense of well-being. The study of interhuman relationships in the 1960s led to a preoccupation with ideas of "urban living" and "spatial cities". In those days, I jokingly used the expression "socio-realism".

In the wake of the oil crisis of the 1970s, when the finite nature of fossil fuels was brought home to us and we became aware that we were endangering the very existence of our earth in continuing to exploit them, we devoted our attention to energy-saving forms of building. Now ecology is the vital issue of the day.

Is this, then, the age of eco-realism? Are biological and social factors passé?

Of course they are not. They are not just passing trends, ephemeral "-isms" of our cultural history. We are confronted with permanent realities that will be of continuing concern to us in the coming millennium. The body of knowledge that will play a decisive role in the architecture of the future is expanding all the time. This is what I call "Real Architecture". As far as I am concerned, architecture is not some formal fashion associated with a particular period. It is a social contract to create buildings and cities based on as much information as possible about the state and feelings of man in various spaces and in different climatic zones. It has to do with the situations that are conducive to human relations and with the compatibility of artificial (i.e. built) intrusions upon the environment.

Since the research course "Real Architecture" was set up at the Academy for Fine Arts in Munich, we have devoted a great deal of thought to these matters. Seven main areas of study have been established that may be summarized under the following headings.

Location:
showing consideration for and setting new accents in the existing building fabric or the landscape.
Climate:
dependence on the conditions of a specific climatic zone.
Nature:
reciprocal relationships between nature, man and architecture.
Technology:
the application of modern technologies.
Means:
the development and use of appropriate economic resources.
Communication:
providing architectural options for the community.
The individual:
the physical and emotional needs of the individual.

We have come to realize that, in designing a building, all these factors and all relevant information must be brought to bear at the same time, even if they may not all possess the same degree of significance. This reflects the relationship between the seven main factors described above, which may be expressed in the form of the diagram on page 5.

In taking these factors into account in the planning stage, the latest knowledge in a particular field will be implemented in the form of basic principles.

After 15 years' work at the Academy in Munich, we recently analysed the comprehensiveness and modern-day relevance of these factors in a seminar lasting two terms. We came to the conclusion that there was no longer so much talk of building for the community. Instead, the state of the individual had now assumed central importance.

The architectural scene is dominated by modern technologies; but there is little information on the role played by nature in our planned environment. Another aspect of equal significance is the influence of the location, where a new trend towards simplification seems to be manifesting itself. Coupled with this, however, an element of monumentality may be discerned that appears to show little respect for the determinant existing building fabric and the landscape. There is a growing awareness of the importance of using appropriate means, but the increasing complexity of building technology and an enormous tide of regulations represent an almost insurmountable barrier to simplicity. A new factor - the influence of electronics and microbiology - has appeared on the horizon, as well as the effects of various patterns of migration. We have also discussed the effects of electronics in different realms of building design, and we have asked ourselves whether we are not on the threshold of an age of "virtual architecture".

The influence of modern transmission media and planning techniques is undeniable. The computer workplace in the home and the fax machine may ultimately reduce road traffic, but are they conducive to human relations? Perhaps residential areas will soon be equipped with communications labs to compensate for this; and possibly media communications will help realize the dream of the decentralized comprehensive school. The introduction of the computer into the realm of design and its faculty for repetition and speeding up the whole process have led to a loss of innovation and to simplification in comparison with conventional methods. Caution is required in this respect, however, for some computer freaks are veritable geniuses in the use of these electronic instruments. Since children are growing up with this technology today, future generations may be able to use a mouse with as much facility as we do a pencil and sketch pad.

At this juncture, however, it is necessary to question the whole world of virtual reality; to regard "Real Architecture" - which should not be confused with the realistic world of building - as a true challenge and to cultivate a more intense use of the principles listed above.

The main principles of "Real Architecture" are described in this book through the projects, in which substance and meaning play a major role. In addition, an indication is given of where a particular principle manifests itself in other projects. In this way, the holistic system of "Real Architecture" in the developmental process of design will be demonstrated by means of actual built examples. No claim can be made to having presented a complete picture, since new information and insights are constantly coming to light.

Many architects today are concerned with similar matters, although they do not follow the systematic method of "Real Architecture". We, too, proceed in an intuitive way in many cases; but the circle of relationships used as a test of comprehensiveness often leads to fuller results, and not infrequently, these deviate from formal trends. Even if we are working intensively to find forms for existing or predetermined functions, design without content is something alien to us.

Erich Schneider–Wessling □ □ □

Ort ■ *Location*

Architektur ist immer Teil des Kontextes, bestimmt ihn, leitet sich aus ihm ab, antwortet. In einer starken Umgebung, an einem durch regionale Eigenheiten oder historisch stark geprägten Ort, der sein eigenes Gesicht hat, gilt es den Geist aufzuspüren, ihn zu interpretieren, zu steigern.

Dem nicht so eindeutig definierten Kontext, dort, wo ratlose Haltlosigkeit herrscht und die Spuren verwischt sind, kann ein starkes Zeichen einen Impuls geben und Identifikation schaffen, die der Beliebigkeit das Spezifische entgegengesetzt, den Raum und den Ort definiert, ein Gefüge akzentuiert. ■ *Architecture always forms part of a certain context. It determines the context and is, in turn, derived from it, is a response to it. In surroundings with a striking identity, in a location that has strong regional or historical features or a bold character of its own, one has to identify the genius loci and interpret and intensify it in new design work.*

Where the context is not so well defined, where the forms are blurred and indistinct and there is a baffling absence of any terms of reference, setting a bold sign can give a fresh impetus and establish a sense of identity and place, counteracting the random with the specific, lending definition to space and location, and generating a new local structure. ▫ ▫ ▫

1.

1. Ein neues Stadtökotop nimmt mit Bezugskomponenten die Umgebung auf: Wasserkanäle des Niederrheins, Windskulpturen, und typische Pflanzen und Tiere. ■ *A new urban "ecotope" enters into a dialogue with the surrounding areas through various points of reference: waterways fed by the lower Rhine, wind sculptures and the typical flora and fauna of the area.*

2. Der 150 Jahre alte Baumbestand des Parks einer Villa setzt die Maßstäbe und fordert behutsames Einfügen; das Gebäude schmiegt sich in die Nischen und schwingt sich um die Bäume herum. ■ *The 150-year-old stock of trees in the park-like grounds of a villa set the scale for this project and required a careful integration of the new development. The sinuous line of the building nestles into hollows and winds itself around the group of trees.*

3. Die Elemente: Bayer-Hochaus, Carl-Duisberg-Park und Japanischer Garten bestimmen den Ort, das neue Kommunikationszentrum verlangt zurückhaltende Einbindung. ■ *The Bayer tower block, the Carl Duisberg Park and the Japanese garden are the dominant elements of this location. The new communication centre required an unobtrusive integration into the existing context.*

4. Die vorhandene Bebauung der Umgebung wird respektiert. Dies macht die Veränderung des Bebauungsplanes von geschlossener Blockbauweise zu offenen Häusern erforderlich. ■ *The existing pattern of building in this area was respected. This required a change in the development plan from a closed street block layout to an open form of construction.*

5. In einem polymorphen Gewerbegebiet ohne Bedingungen an formales Einfügen beschränkt sich das Gebäude auf die inneren Funktionen und den Akzent des Treppenturmes; der Unort ist geblieben. ■ *In a heterogeneous area of light industry with no points of reference for a formal integration of new developments, the building confines itself to an expression of the internal functions with the staircase tower forming a salient feature; the locational vacuum remains.*

6. Eine gesichtslose Straße aus der Nachkriegszeit im Süden von Köln bekommt eine „Nase". ■ *A faceless, post-war street development in south Cologne is given a "nose".*

7. Der Ort ist durch die vielgestaltige Welt eines urbanen Hinterhofes bestimmt, es gilt die Verhältnisse zu nutzen. ■ *The challenge of this location was to exploit the heterogeneous world of an inner-city rear courtyard as fully as possible.*

2.
3.
4.

5.
6.
7.

Neue Stadtmitte, Kaarst ■ *New Civic Centre, Kaarst*

Der Stadt Kaarst, als Schlafstadt von Düsseldorf in den vergangenen 30 Jahren auf ca. 40.000 Einwohner angewachsen, fehlt in ihrem Gefüge ein Kristallisationspunkt, der die Kraft und Dynamik in sich birgt, ihr Selbstbewußtsein zu geben und über die Innenstadt hinaus in die heterogen strukturierte Umgebung auszustrahlen.

Durch ein markantes Zeichen bekommt der undefinierte Ort Identifikation und Unverwechselbarkeit für die Kaarster Bürger: Ein Ensemble aus Rathaus, Bürgerhaus und Marktplatz mit Geschäftszentrum übernimmt diese Aufgabe.

Das Konzept, als Ergebnis eines Wettbewerbs entstanden, sieht Einzelgebäude vor, die ihre Funktionen klar nach außen definieren: ein mehrgeschossiges Rathaus mit den traditionellen Elementen Halle und Turm, ein niedrigeres Clubhaus mit vorgelagerter Wasserfläche und - für eine mögliche Erweiterung vorgesehen - ein dreischiffiges Bürgerhaus. Optische und räumliche Kontinuität erhält die Gebäudegruppe durch nur leicht variierte Dachformen und ein umlaufendes Band von Foyers und Arkaden. Erweitert um einen Geschäftshauskomplex entsteht ein allseitig geschlossener Platz als neue Stadtmitte.

In Verbindung mit der sich südlich anschließenden Grünanlage mit bewußt artifiziell gehaltener Wasserführung und vielfältigem Freizeitangebot entsteht ein attraktiver öffentlicher Raum, der als innerstädtisches Ökotop die lebendige Einheit von Stadt und Landschaft, von Zivilisation und Natur für den Bürger erlebbar macht.

1. Die neue Stadtmitte mit Rathaus, Bürgerhaus, Geschäftszentrum und Café und der Park werden zu einem Gesamtkunstwerk und bringen die Ansprüche von Natur und Zivilisation, die heute so konträr zueinander stehen, in einen interessanten, einmaligen und harmonischen Einklang. ■ *The new civic centre with town hall, civic amenities building, commercial centre, café and park is conceived as a Gesamtkunstwerk that seeks to reconcile the apparently conflicting present-day claims of nature and civilization, uniting them in a unique and fascinating state of harmony.*

1.

Lageplan ■ *Site plan*
1. Rathaus, 2. Bürgerhaus, 3. Theater
4. Geschäftszentrum, 5. Café ■
1. Town hall, 2. Civic amenities building, 3. Theatre, 4. Commercial centre, 5. Café

Das Rathaus

Der obligatorische Turm wie aus einem Kinderbaukasten ist ein eindeutiges Zeichen in der Stadt, und er markiert den Eingang des Rathauses. Eine Halle verschafft dem Bürger den Durchblick durch den Ämterwald und dem Bürgermeister den Überblick.

In den Außenbereichen die Büros, um das Treppenhaus die allgemeinen Dienste vom Kopierer zum WC; die Turmzimmer sind für jeden da, als Besprechungsräume, an höchster Stelle der Hochzeitssaal und die Aussichtsterrasse, im Untergeschoß befindet sich eine Artothek und die Bibliothek, im obersten Geschoß ist die Chefetage. Das Treppenhaus ist ein kommunikatives Element in der Halle und im Turm. Zusätzliche Treppen am Ende der Korridore verbinden Abteilungen vertikal. Die Büroetagen lassen sich in Kombibüros für mehr Mitarbeiter umwandeln.

Die Halle wurde mit genügend automatischen Fensteröffnungen und Sonnenschutzsegeln versehen und bildet so einen sehr effizienten Beitrag zur Energieersparnis. Eine gute Belichtung und Abstandsflächen werden dadurch erreicht, daß das Dachgeschoß zurückgesetzt ist. Die Stahlskelettkonstruktion und weite Fensteröffnungen mit Blickbezug zur Straße erzeugen eine freundliche Atmosphäre für die Mitarbeiter. Bredero zu Titanzinkblech und weiße Markisen prägen das Erscheinungsbild.

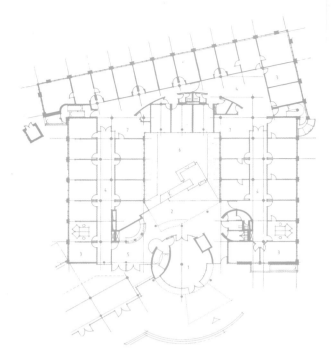

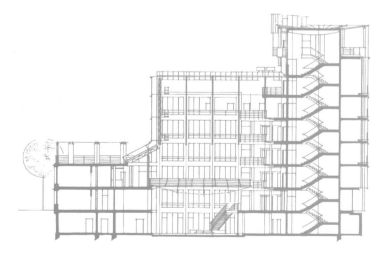

5.

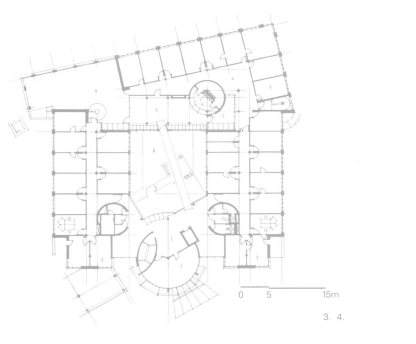

1. Der obligatorische Turm ist ein eindeutiges Zeichen in der Stadt, und er markiert den Eingang des Rathauses. ■ *The obligatory tower is a clear emblem of the town and marks the entrance to the town hall.*

2. Rathausturm und Halle von Norden. ■ *View of tower and town hall from the north.*

3. Erdgeschoß ■ *Ground floor plan*
   1. Windfang ■ *Windtrap*
   2. Foyer ■ *Foyer*
   3. Büro ■ *Office*
   4. Flur ■ *Corridor*
   5. Infothek ■ *Information desk*
   6. Halle ■ *Hall*
   7. Spielraum / Wartehalle ■ *Waiting room*

4. Obergeschoß ■ *First floor plan*
   1. Galerie ■ *Gallery*
   2. Besprechung ■ *Conference room*
   3. Büro ■ *Office*
   4. Flur ■ *Corridor*
   5. Kantine ■ *Cantine*
   6. Küche ■ *Kitchen*
   7. Innenhof ■ *Courtyard*
   8. Luftraum-Halle ■ *Light well*
   9. Terrasse ■ *Terrace*

5. Schnitt ■ *Section*

Landschaftsplanung

Entgegen einer zielgerichteten und geordneten Bebauung entwickelte sich der Ortsteil Kaarst am Rande des Ballungszentrums Düsseldorf zufällig. Die dadurch entstandene Heterogenität der Bebauung weist kaum ein übergeordnetes und für ein Gemeinwesen wichtiges Identifikationsmerkmal auf.

Es ist besonders deshalb unverzichtbar, einen für die Kaarster Bürger attraktiven Identifikationsbereich zu entwickeln. Das Ziel war, einen Stadtkern zu schaffen, der über Kaarst hinaus Bedeutung gewinnt. Die Ortskernbebauung und der Park sind zu einem Gesamtkunstwerk entwickelt worden, das die Ansprüche von Natur und Zivilisation, die heute so konträr zueinander stehen, in einen interessanten, einmaligen und harmonischen Einklang bringt.

1.

2.  3. 4.

Die Markthalle

Die Architekten haben das Wort „Super-Markt" wörtlich genommen. Eine lebendige, lichtdurchflutete Atmosphäre des Markts mit vielen Läden ist eine Attraktion selbst für Düsseldorf. Zusammen mit dem Freiflächenkonzept und der guten Erreichbarkeit mit dem Pkw wird dadurch Kaufkraft gebunden und gar von auswärts angezogen.

Es kann in dem Geviert auch ein ganz konventioneller Lebensmittelmarkt untergebracht werden mit Läden drum herum, in dem Obergeschoß der Oberstadt Parkplätze für die Kunden, an den Außenseiten Wohnungen oder Büros.

Das Maubiszentrum wird durch 4-geschossige Bauten ergänzt, so daß sich dem Rathaus gegenüber ein ruhiger Stadtraum ergibt. Für die Wohngebäude wurde eine Tiefgarage angelegt. ▫ ▫ ▫

1. Die Rathaushalle: Die Treppe und die gläserne Brücke sind kommunikative Elemente und können - wie bei der Einweihung geschehen - als offene Bühnen bespielt werden. ■ *Large central space in town hall: the staircase and glass bridge are communicational elements that can also be used as an open stage, as at the inauguration ceremony*

2. Eine der beiden Außentreppen. ■ *One of the two external staircases.*

3. Unterspannte filigrane Konstruktionen des Hallentragwerkes und der Brückenkonstruktion. Beton, Stahl und Glas sind die wesentlichen Materialien. ■ *The bridge structure and the filigree roof construction over the hall, with trusses tensioned on the underside; the principal materials are concrete, steel and glass.*

4. Das Treppenauge. ■ *Stairwell*

5. Die fünfgeschossige Rathaushalle, ein überdachter Platz, verbindet die beiden Bürohäuser. Der gläserne Himmel überdacht den inneren Platz und schützt vor dem rauhen Klima. Vor Überhitzung im Sommer schützen Sonnensegel als künstliche Wolken. ■ *The five-storey central space of the town hall building. This covered public square links the two office tracts and is sheltered against the vagaries of the weather by a "sky of glass". Solar sails like artificial clouds provide protection against overheating in summer.*

5.

Kaarst is a dormitory town outside Düsseldorf with a population that has grown to approximately 40,000 in the last 30 years. The urban fabric, however, lacks a focal point with the power and dynamics to generate a sense of civic pride and to radiate its presence beyond the local centre to the heterogeneous surrounding areas. With the creation of a bold urban development of symbolic importance, this ill-defined place was to be given an unmistakable character and a new sense of identity for the citizens of Kaarst. The new ensemble consists of a town hall, a civic amenities building, a market place and commercial centre.

The concept, which was the outcome of a competition, foresaw a number of individual buildings, the functions of which would be clearly defined on the outside. These include a multi-storey town hall with the traditional elements of a hall and tower, a lower club house with an area of water in front of it, and a three-bay civic centre, to be realized at a later date. The ensemble derives its quality of visual and spatial continuity from the similar but slightly varied roof forms and a peripheral strip accommodating foyers and arcades. Complemented by commercial and shopping facilities, the complex forms a new town centre laid out about a civic square that is closed on all sides.

Together with the adjoining landscaped open space to the south, with the evidently artificial lake and waterways, and a broad range of leisure facilities, the square represents an attractive "ecotope" at the very heart of the community, affording the inhabitants the experience of a living unity of town and landscape, civilization and nature.

1.
1. Das „Bootshaus" - das Café - zwischen kleinem Bürgerhaus und Geschäftszentrum. ■ The "Boathouse": the café between the small civic amenities building and the commercial and housing centre.

2. 3. 4.
Das Wasser verbindet zwischen stadträumlicher Dichte und freier Parklandschaft. ■ Water forms the link between intense urban development and the open park landscape.

5. Geschäftszentrum Obergeschoß. ■ Commercial and housing centre, upper floor.

6. Geschäftszentrum Erdgeschoß. ■ Commercial and housing centre, ground floor.

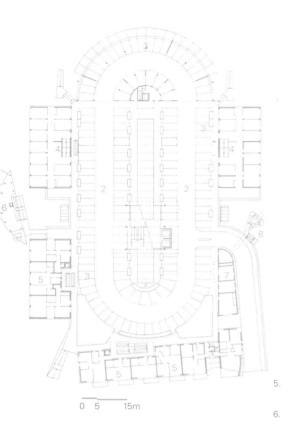

Oberstadt ■ *Upper town*
1. Markthalle ■ *Market hall*
2. Straße ■ *Street*
3. Parken ■ *Parking*
4. Büros ■ *Offices*
5. Wohnungen ■ *Apartments*
6. Café ■ *Café*
7. Technikzentrale ■ *Technic*
8. Werbeturm ■ *Advertising tower*

Erdgeschoß ■ *Ground floor*
1. Markthalle ■ *Merket hall*
2. Arkade ■ *Arcade*
3. Café ■ *Café*
4. Supermarkt ■ *Super market*
5. Läden ■ *Shops*
6. Wohnungen ■ *Apartments*
7. See ■ *Lake*

Town hall

The obligatory tower, as it might be visualized by a child with a set of building blocks, becomes a clear emblem of the community and marks the location of the entrance to the town hall.

A central hall allows citizens a clearer view through the maze of official departments and also helps the mayor to keep track of what is going on in his own house. The offices are located in the peripheral areas. General service facilities, from photocopying to WCs, are grouped around the staircase. The rooms in the tower are accessible to everyone as areas for consultation and meetings. The room at the top is reserved for civil marriages and has a viewing terrace.

An artotheque and library are accommodated in the basement. The heads of department have their offices on the top floor. The staircase functions as a communicational element in the hall and the tower. Additional stairs at the ends of the corridors create vertical links between departments. The administrative storeys can be converted into combination offices for more employees.

The hall is equipped with an adequate number of automatically opening casements and with sunscreen sails. It thus makes an extremely efficient contribution to the programme of energy conservation. Good natural lighting and the statutory distances from neighbouring buildings are achieved by setting back the top storey.

A steel skeleton frame structure and large window openings affording views to the street help to create a friendly atmosphere for the staff. The overall appearance is distinguished by the use of precast concrete units, titanium-zinc sheeting and white blinds.

1. Wohn- und Bürogebäude und der obere Eingang zur Markthalle definieren die „Oberstadt". ■ The "upper town" contains housing and offices and the upper entrance to the market hall.

2. Eine lichtdurchflutete Markthalle mit vielen Läden. ■ The bright market hall with a large range of shops.

3. 4. Die Wohnbauten de Oberstadt. ■ Housing in the "upper town".

Market hall

The architects took the word "super-market" literally, creating the lively, brightly lit atmosphere of a market with a large number of shops in a development that forms an attraction even for the citizens of Düsseldorf.

This concept, together with the design of the outdoor spaces and the easy accessibility for cars, makes the market a great magnet for local shoppers and spending power and also attracts visitors from further afield. A conventional food market can be accommodated within the complex with shops around the edges. At the top of the "upper town" are customers' parking spaces, with dwellings or offices on the outer faces. The Maubis Centre is complemented by four-storey housing and commercial structures that create a peaceful urban space opposite the town hall. A basement garage was constructed for the housing.

Landscape planning

Situated on the outskirts of the city of Düsseldorf, Kaarst was not subject to any consistent programme of planning, but underwent a piecemeal, random development. The heterogeneous nature of the settlement reveals virtually none of those salient features that are so important for a community and its sense of identity.

For that reason it was essential to develop an attractive realm with which the citizens of Kaarst would be able to identify. The aim of the project was to create an urban centre that would assume an importance extending beyond the confines of Kaarst itself. The town centre and park have been designed as a Gesamtkunstwerk, a universal work of art that will reconcile the claims of nature and civilization - which have become such opposites today - and unite them in a unique and fascinating state of harmony.

3.
4.

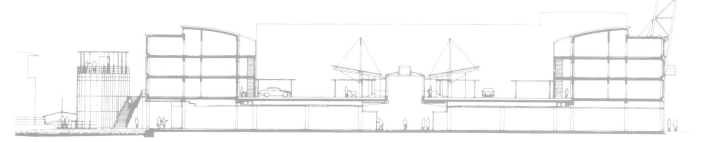

Klima ■ *Climate*

Unser Verhalten wird auch von den klimatischen Verhältnissen bestimmt, in denen wir leben, ist Reaktion auf die Konditionen unserer Umwelt. So entstehen Besonderheiten und Gewohnheiten als Prozesse von Anpassungen, die, wie unser Klima, Wandlungen unterliegen. Die vorrangige Forderung an Gebautes besteht darin, uns vor den Einflüssen des Klimas zu schützen. Daraus entstehen Bauformen, die ihre Entsprechung in den Nutzformen finden.

Wir ziehen uns im Winter zurück und breiten uns im Sommer aus. Die Raumformen für die ausgiebigen Übergangszeiten in unseren gemäßigten Zonen um den 50. Breitengrad bilden die „Zwischenräume" zwischen innen und außen, als zweite Häute, Membranen unserer Ausdehnung. Wintergärten in den privaten Bereichen, und im städtischen Kontext verglaste, überdachte öffentliche Räume erlauben uns die Anpassung an unsere Umwelt. Durch den technischen Fortschritt der Glasherstellung und -verarbeitung und neuartiger Regel- und Steuerungstechniken unterstützt, entstehen neue Bau- und Lebensformen. ■

Our behaviour is also influenced by the climatic conditions in which we live. It is a reaction to the factors determining our environment. Special characteristics and habits develop as part of the process of adjustment to these conditions, and they, too, are subject to change like the weather. The first requirement of a building is that it should protect us from the elements. This results in built forms that reflect functional needs.

In winter, we withdraw indoors; in summer, life expands outwards. The spatial forms we have developed for the lengthy transitional periods in our temperate zones (around 50° latitude) are the "intermediate realms" between inside and outside, a kind of second skin or membrane to accommodate our expansive needs.

Conservatories in the private realm and glass-covered public urban spaces help us to adapt to our environment. New forms of construction and new patterns of living evolve as a result of technical advances in the manufacture and processing of glass and with the development of new automatic control systems.

□ □ □

1.

1. Die Bäume verschatten im Sommer, im Winter dringen die Sonnenstrahlen tief ins Haus ein. ■ *The trees provide shade in summer; in winter, the rays of the sun penetrate into the heart of the building.*

2. Der gläserne Himmel überdacht den inneren Platz und schützt vor rauhem Klima, vor Überhitzung im Sommer schützen Sonnensegel als künstliche Wolken. ■ *A sky of glass is drawn over the internal space and protects it against vagaries of the weather. Solar sails like artificial clouds provide protection against overheating in summer.*

3. Das Zuluftbauwerk dreht sich in den Wind und belüftet den unterirdischen Multifunktionsraum auf natürliche Weise. ■ *The air-intake structure turns in the wind, drawing air by natural means into the underground multi-purpose space below.*

4. Kompakte Bauweise, große Haustiefen. ■ *Compact form of construction with greater building depths.*

5. Große Gebäudetiefen mit wenig Abstrahlungsflächen. ■ *Great building depths with fewer surfaces for emissive energy losses.*

6. Ergänzung durch Aufstockung, Erweiterung der Halle und zwei Wohnungen mit Südorientierung auf dem Dachgeschoß. ■ *Scope for extension in the form of an additional storey, the enlargement of the hall, and two south-facing flats in the attic storey.*

7. Verwendung von ökologisch vertretbaren Materialien. ■ *Use of ecologically sustainable materials.*

2. 3. 4.

5 6 7

Deutsche Bundesstiftung Umwelt, Osnabrück ■ *Federal German Foundation for the Environment, Osnabrück*

Die besondere Form des Gebäudes ist das Ergebnis der Rücksichtnahme gegenüber der natürlichen Situation einer Parklandschaft im Villenviertel mit zwei- bis dreigeschossiger Bebauung. Sie ist zudem Ausdruck einer energiebewußten Architekturauffassung und soll die Aufgaben des Umweltinstituts repräsentieren und symbolisieren. Das gläserne Gebäude fügt sich nahtlos in den Park ein. Es folgt den Baumkonturen, umschließt die imposante 150 Jahre alte Buchengruppe als Mittelpunkt und verwandelt so den Außenraum zum Innenhof.

Die Fassade, eine vollverglaste Holz/Alukonstruktion, wird von einem leichten Rankgerüst begleitet, das durch die Bepflanzung den natürlichen Sonnenschutz garantiert. Ergänzt mit Glaselementen können im Sinne einer doppelten Fassade Wintergärten mit Pufferfunktion entstehen.

Durch die radiale Anordnung entwickeln sich im Inneren die Räume zu dynamisch enger und weiter werdenden Raumfolgen, die ideal für Kombizonen geeignet sind. „Sonnenfänger" über den Mittelpunkten der Ringe leiten das Licht tief ins Gebäude hinein und durchlichten auf natürliche Weise. Auf Kunstlicht kann im Tagesgang verzichtet werden.

1. Der Konferenzraum im Osten. ■ *The conference hall to the east.*

2. Ein Band schlängelt sich durch den Park und umrahmt eine Gruppe von 150 Jahre alten imposanten Buchen. ■ *Like a ribbon, the building winds its way through the park, framing a magnificent group of 150-year-old beech trees.*

3. Ein exponiertes Stahltragwerk ermöglicht den stützenfreien Konferenzraum. ■ *The form of the exposed steel structure enabled the conference hall to be built without intermediate columns.*

An den minimierten Nordseiten liegen die Eingangshalle, die Treppenhäuser und Nebenräume. Kurze Wege im Inneren verringern Verkehrsflächen, erzeugen Kompaktheit und lassen große Flexibilität zu. ◻ ◻ ◻

Energiekonzept
- Die Kreisform ermöglicht ein kompaktes Gebäude mit einem günstigen Verhältnis von Außenhülle zu Kubatur.
- Durch Verzicht auf eine Tiefgarage bzw. ein Untergeschoß wird der Baumbestand geschont.
- Vollverglaste Fassaden mit hochwärmegedämmten Fenstern mit Dreifachverglasung mit Argon gefüllt und metall-oxydbeschichtet (0,8 W/m² K) führen zu einer positiven Energiebilanz.
- Die mechanische, benutzerkontrollierte Lüftung, basierend auf Gegenstromlüftung nach dem Schwerkraftprinzip, erlaubt auf eine Klimaanlage zu verzichten.
- Die gute Tageslichtsituation, unterstützt durch die Lichttürme in den Zentren des Gebäudes, gewährleistet an 80% aller Stunden des Jahres in der Zeit zwischen 9.00 Uhr und 17.00 Uhr die geforderte Nennbelichtungsstärke von 300 Lux am Arbeitsplatz.
- Solarkollektoren für Warmwasser.
- Photovoltaik zur Stromerzeugung und Steuerungstechnik, über Chipkarten geregelt, senkt den Energieverbrauch.

1. 2. 3. 4.
5.

- Abfallarme Bauproduktion und recyclinggerechte Baukonstruktionen vermeiden Abfallmengen im Bauwesen und schonen die Resourcen:

    Recyclingbeton in den tragenden Wänden, erstmals bei einem Hochbauvorhaben in Deutschland eingesetzt;

    Schaumglasdämmung unter der Bodenplatte und im Dach;

    Isofloc-Dämmung aus Altpapier in den Innenwänden; möglichst keine Verwendung von Verbundsystemen zwischen Rohbau und Ausbau;

    kompostierbare Naturfaserteppiche;

    Bodenplatten aus Recyclingmaterial;

    Naturfarben für Holzanstriche.

Erdgeschoß ■ *Ground floor plan*
1. Foyer ■ *Foyer*
2. Cafeteria ■ *Cafeteria*
3. Küche ■ *Kitchen*
4. Terrasse ■ *Patio*
5. Besprechung ■ *Discussion room*
6. Konferenz ■ *Conference room*
7. Bibliothek ■ *Library*
8. Gang zur Villa ■ *Corridor to villa*
9. WC ■ *WC*
10. Beh.-WC ■ *Disabled persons' WC*
11. Lager ■ *Store*
12. Entsorgung ■ *Waste disposal*
13. Anlieferung ■ *Deliveries*
14. Werkstatt ■ *Workshop*
15. Büro ■ *Office*
16. Hausmeister ■ *Caretaker*

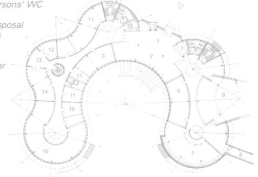

0   5   10   15m

1. Die zweite Haut des Gebäudes für Bepflanzung und Wintergarten-Verglasung. ■ *The second skin of the building for plants and conservatory glazing.*

3. Das Laub der Bäume als natürlicher Sonnenschutz. ■ *The foliage of the trees provides natural solar shading.*

2. 4. Der Außenraum wird zum Innenhof. ■ *The external space is enclosed by the building to form a sheltered courtyard.*

5. Die Eingangsseite im Norden mit minimierten Öffnungen für Nebenräume. ■ *The north-facing entrance front with a minimum of openings for ancillary spaces.*

Obergeschoß ■ *Upper floor plan*
1. Kopierraum ■ *Photocopying*
2. Teeküche ■ *Kitchenette*
3. WC ■ *WC*
4. Lager ■ *Store*
5. Büro ■ *Office*
6. Flur ■ *Corridor*
7. Luftraum ■ *Light well*

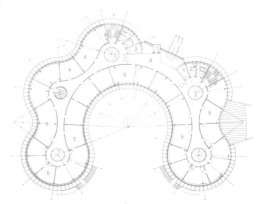

1.2.
Verlängert nach innen, decken die Gitterroste einen umlaufenden Installationskanal ab, der flexible Raumaufteilung ermöglicht. ■ *Extended into the interior, the metal gratings are laid over a peripheral services duct, which facilitates a flexible division of space.*

3. Keine Flure, sondern interessante Raumfolgen zwischen den Büros. ■ *Interesting sequences of spaces instead of corridors between offices.*

4. Die Eingangshalle. ■ *The entrance hall.*

5. Kleine Plätze vor den Büros. ■ *Small, varied spaces outside offices.*

6. Die Sonnentürme fangen trotz des verschatteten Grundstücks durch die hohe Lage und durch die Ausrichtung optimal Sonnenlicht und Energie für die Innenzonen ein. ■ *Through their elevated position and orientation, the solar stacks catch an optimum amount of sunlight and energy for the inner zones of the building, despite the shady nature of the site.*

1.

2.

The distinctive form of the building reflects the role played by the natural environment in the design considerations. Set in a park-like situation in an exclusive residential area with two- and three-storey villa developments, the building is also an expression of an energy-conscious attitude towards architecture. At the same time, it was meant to represent and symbolize the objectives of this institute for environmental matters. The glass structure is perfectly assimilated into the park. Its form echoes the outlines of the trees and encloses a magnificent 160-year-old group of beeches at the centre, transforming the external space into a secluded courtyard.

The façade is a fully-glazed timber and aluminium construction. Drawn over it is a light trellis-work for climbing plants, which guarantee a natural form of solar shading.

In conjunction with glazed elements, a double-layer façade can be created with conservatory areas that function as a buffer zone.

The radial layout results in a sequence of dynamically tapering and expanding internal spaces that are ideally suited to accommodate a mixture of uses. "Sun traps" above the centres of the circular sections allow light to penetrate deep into the building and illuminate it naturally. During daylight hours, artificial lighting is not necessary.

Situated along the restrained north faces of the development are the entrance hall, staircases and ancillary spaces. Short internal routes help to reduce the circulation areas to a minimum, create a quality of compactness and permit a high degree of flexibility.

3.   4.   5.   6.

Energy concept
- Circular forms result in a compact volume with a favourable relationship between the area of the external skin and the cubic content.
- The decision not to build an underground garage or basement enabled the stock of trees to be preserved.
- Fully glazed façades with a high degree of thermal insulation - metallic-oxide-coated, argon-filled triple glazing (0.8 W/m2K) - help to create a positive energy balance.
- A mechanical ventilation system, controlled by the users and based on a gravity-regulated counter-current principle, makes it possible to do without air-conditioning.
- Good daylight conditions, supported by the light stacks in the middle of the building, guarantee the required nominal level of illumination for workplaces (300 lux) for 80 per cent of all hours of the year between 9 a.m. and 5 p.m.
- Hot water is supplied from solar collectors.
- Electricity obtained from a photovoltaic installation, together with microchip control technology, reduces energy supply needs.
- Low-waste building products and recyclable forms of construction help to avoid waste in the building industry and conserve resources:
    recycled concrete in the load-bearing walls, used for the first time in a building project in Germany;
    foamed glass insulation under the floor slab and in the roof;
    Iso-Floc insulation, consisting of recycled paper, in internal partitions;
    minimum use of constructional bonding between structure and finishings;
    biodegradable natural-fibre carpeting;
    floor slabs made of recycled materials;
    use of natural substances for painting woodwork.

Natur einschalten ■ *Restoring the natural environment*

1.

Das Bauen richtet sich immer gegen die Natur, es entreißt ihr Lebensraum, es fügt ihr Wunden zu. Doch wir Menschen sind auch ein Teil von ihr, leben in ihr und mit ihr. In der Sehnsucht nach der natürlichen Umwelt, nach Kontakt zur Landschaft, nach „Grün", das sich in vielfältiger Weise äußert, scheint sich ein Grundbedürfnis des Menschen zu manifestieren. Dies nicht zu berücksichtigen, führt zu beschädigtem Leben.

So müssen wir das, was wir der Natur wegnehmen, so weit wie möglich zurückgeben. Versiegelung muß reduziert werden, Gärten, Dachgärten, „grüne Zimmer", Begrünung von Häusern, grüne Netze und Parks sind unverzichtbare Elemente in unserem städtischen Lebensraum. ■

The act of building is always contrary to nature. It tears a piece of habitat from the natural world and inflicts wounds on it. But man is also part of nature; he lives with it and within it. Our yearning for the natural environment, for contact with the landscape, for the countryside and verdant nature manifests itself in many different ways and is an expression of a basic human need. To ignore it is to impair life.

For that reason, it is necessary to restore to nature as much as possible of what we have taken from it. The sealing off of our habitat must be reduced. Gardens, roof gardens, "green rooms", the planting of buildings, landscaped networks and parks are indispensable elements in our urban habitat. ▫ ▫ ▫

2.

3.

4.

5.

6.

1. Die Rankgerüste, der See und die begrünte Dachlandschaft verflechten Gebautes und Natur. ■ *The lake, the plants climbing up the trellis-work, and the landscaped roofs achieve an interweaving of nature and buildings.*

2. Das Gegensatzpaar Stadt-Landschaft wird durch die Kommunikations- und Wasserachse verknüpft. Das „Öko"-Kaarst wird im weitesten Sinne als Einheit von Kernbebauung und Landschaftspark verstanden. ■ *The contrasting environents of city and country are here linked by conceptual axes in the form of communication and water. The ecological environment of Kaarst is comprehended as a unity of core development and landscaped park.*

3. Vegetation als Sonnenschutz; das Gebäude wird Teil des Parks. ■ *Vegetation as a form of solar shading; the building merges into the park.*

4. Die üppige Begrünung an der Fassade und auf dem Dach läßt auch mitten in der Stadt die Natur spüren. ■ *The profuse planting of the façades and the roof bring a touch of nature to the centre of the city.*

5. Anlage eines Netzparks, in dem die Innenhöfe mit den öffentlichen Grünflächen verflochten werden. ■ *Creation of a park-like network in which courtyard spaces are interwoven with public landscaped areas.*

6. Der kleine Hof mit der Birke und den Rankpflanzen schafft eine Beziehung zum Außenraum. ■ *The small courtyard with the birch tree and climbing plants creates a link with the outdoor world.*

Kommunikationszentrum der Bayer AG, Leverkusen ■ *Bayer AG Communication Centre, Leverkusen*

Als Ergebnis eines Wettbewerbes ist das Begegnungs- und Ausstellungsgebäude der Bayer AG ein modernes Kommunikationszentrum mit dem Anspruch, zu repräsentieren und neu überdachte Werte der Großchemie zu vermitteln.

Ziel der Planung war es, die Fläche zwischen dem dominanten 31-geschossigen Bayer-Verwaltungshochhaus, Carl-Duisberg-Park und Japanischem Garten baulich so zu nutzen, daß sowohl eine Abrundung des Parks nach Westen als auch eine harmonische Verzahnung der bestehenden Geländeelemente gelingt. Das mit seiner Hauptfront nach Westen orientierte Gebäude schiebt sich, teilweise 3-geschossig, so in das 3 m nach Süden abfallende Gelände, daß die Dachzone zum begehbaren Park und die Fassade zur Architekturkante wird, die den Landschaftsstrich akzentuiert.

Das um 1,20 m abgesenkte Rondell mit seinen Arenastufen und einer dem Kreisrund folgenden Rampe schafft eine klare lebendige Eingangssituation, und großzügige Rampenhöhen im ebenerdigen Bereich. Über ein Foyer mit Cafeteria erschließen sich die verschiedenen Bereiche des Gebäudes, ein arenaförmig abgesunkener Multifunktionsraum, vier Konferenzräume im 2. Untergeschoß, Büros für die Werksführung und der Ausstellungspavillon. Eine Glas-pyramide deckt das Zentrum des quadratischen Baus. Den gläsernen Fronten der Halle ist ein von schlanken Säulen getragener Umgang mit Rankgerüsten und einer Laube vorgelagert. Die Grenzen zwischen innen und außen lösen sich auf. Die Wechselbeziehung von Mensch, Natur und Architektur erhält eine besondere Qualität.

1. Drei Elemente der Dachlandschaft: Bogenträger, Glaspyramide und Zuluftbauwerk.
Der Bogenträger überspannt den unterirdischen Multifunktionsraum. Der bewegliche Lüftungsturm dreht sich in den Wind und klimatisiert den Multifunktionsraum auf natürliche Weise. ■ *Three elements on the landscaped roof: bowstring girder, glass pyramid and air-intake stack. The bowstring girder is spanned over the underground multi-purpose space. The air-intake stack turns in the wind and supplies fresh air to the multi-purpose space by natural means.*

Der architektonische Wille, „der Natur zurückgegeben, was ihr durch Bauen genommen wurde", artikuliert sich in vorrangig funktionalen Elementen der Dachlandschaft: der Glaspyramide der Austellungshalle, dem Bogenträger über dem Multifunktionsraum und dem Zuluftbauwerk, dessen Haube sich selbsttätig in den Wind dreht und diesen durch den Schlot in die Klimaanlage drückt. ▫ ▫ ▫

1. Zurückhaltende Einbindung des neuen Kommunikationszentrums zwischen Bayer-Hochhaus, Carl-Duisberg-Park und Japanischem Garten. ■ *Unobtrusive integration of the new communication centre between the Bayer tower block, the Carl Duisberg Park and the Japanese garden.*

2. Eine besondere Qualität des Herantretens entsteht durch die östliche Wegführung, die den Zugang zentriert: durch das Portal des stählernen Bogens - der Träger der Deckenkonstruktion des darunterliegenden Multifunktionsraumes - über einen segmentförmigen Platz, eine elegant geschwungene Freitreppe und die Rampe hinab auf den Eingangsvorplatz. ■
A special feature of the scheme is the line of access from the east along the entrance axis. Passing through the gateway formed by the steel arch - the roof girder over the multi-purpose space - it leads across a segmental-shaped open area and down an elegantly curving outdoor staircase-ramp to the entrance courtyard.

3. Die Landschaftskante. ■ *Boundary between landscape and architecture.*

4. Die Rankgerüste, der See und die begrünte Dachlandschaft verflechten Gebäude und Natur. ■ *The planted trellis-work, the lake and the landscaped roof interweave building and nature.*

5. Das Eingangsrondell mit dem Vordach. ■ *The circular entrance area and canopy.*

1.

2.
3.
4.
5.

The Bayer AG meeting centre and exhibition hall was the outcome of a successful competition design. It is a modern centre of communication that serves the purposes of self-representation and seeks to convey the new, revised values of the big chemical concerns.

The aim of the planning was to develop the area between the dominant 31-storey Bayer administration tower, the Carl Duisberg Park and the Japanese gardens in such a way that the park would be closed to the west and the existing elements of the site would be harmoniously integrated. The site slopes down to the south with a three-metre difference of level.

The structure with the west-facing main front is three storeys high in part and is built into the slope in such a way that the roof zone can be used as a pedestrian park, while the façade functions as an architectural boundary, accentuating this stretch of the landscape. The circular tract, sunk 1.20 m below ground level, is stepped down in part to form an enclosed arena. A broad, curving ramp creates a clearly articulated, lively entrance situation with generous ramp heights at ground level.

The architectural wish to "restore to nature what building has taken from it" is expressed symbolically in the three sculptural functional elements of the landscaped roof: the glass pyramid over the exhibition hall, the bowstring girder over the multi-purpose space, and the air-supply structure, the hood of which turns in the wind and channels air through a vertical stack to the air-conditioning plant.

Access to the various sections of the building, including the arena-like, sunken multi-purpose space, four conference rooms on the second basement level, offices for the works management, and the exhibition pavilion, is via a foyer with a cafeteria. This square pavilion structure is crowned at the centre by a glass pyramid. Slender columns set in front of the glazed façades of the hall support the projecting roof and form a colonnaded, covered outdoor walkway around the building. Climbing plants growing up the outside on a trellis-work create an additional verdant enclosing layer. The boundary between inside and outside is thus dissolved, and the reciprocal relationships between man, nature and architecture acquire a special quality.

1. Die innenarchitektonische Gestaltung wahrt in ihrer Materialwahl Kontinuität zum Außenraum: Grauwacke, Betonstein und Edelstahl werden zu innenräumlichen Strukturen kombiniert, deren bewußte Sachlichkeit Raum schafft für Lebendigkeit durch Menschen. ■ The choice of materials for the interior design ensures a sense of continuity between indoor and outdoor space: Greywacke sandstone, concrete building blocks and stainless steel are combined to form the internal spatial structures, the deliberate functionality of which allows scope for animation by the people who use these spaces.

2. Der Multifunktionsraum. ■ The multi-purpose space.

3. 4. Der Umgang des Ausstellungspavillions, die Rankgerüste und die Laube: Innen- und Außenraum greifen ineinander und lösen ihre Grenzen auf. ■ The covered walkway around the exhibition pavilion with trellis-work and leafy enclosure: indoor and outdoor space dissolve into each other.

3.

4.

Individualität ■ *Individuality*

Im Erkennen und Erspüren unserer eigenen Bedürfnisse liegt die Herausforderung an unsere gebaute Umwelt. Neben den physischen Bedingungen des gebauten Raumes, uns Schutz und Behaglichkeit zu geben, sind es vor allem die psychischen Faktoren, die uns Spielräume für unser individuelles und soziales Leben bieten sollen. Das Erleben eigener Welten ist Voraussetzung den Anderen und das Andere zu reflektieren und mit der Gemeinschaft in Austausch zu treten.

Wohnen heißt den Raum besetzen und ihn individuell zu beleben, den eigenen Ausdruck zu finden und darzustellen, Freiheit und Geborgenheit erleben zu können in den und durch die „eigenen vier Wände". So gibt es tief in unserem psychischen Empfinden stammesgeschichtlich geprägte Urräume, die vielen Menschen gemein sind, und andere, durch persönliches Erleben erfahrene neue Räume, die individuelle Gefühle evozieren und auslösen können. Sich wandelnde Wohn- und Arbeitsformen durch veränderte Wirtschafts- und Lebensgemeinschaften erfordern offene Strukturen, die dem Einzelnen erlauben, sich nach seinen Wünschen von Privatheit und Gemeinschaft einzurichten. Aktive Teilnahme an der individuellen Gestaltung, persönliche Entfaltung und Mitbestimmung erzeugen größere Identifikation und Nachbarschaftlichkeit. Große Gebäudetiefen, unterschiedliche Geschoßhöhen und Zimmergrößen, unfertige Räume schaffen Wahlfreiheit und Spielräume. ■ *The true challenge facing us in the context of our built environment is to be aware of our own needs and to be able to identify them. In addition to the physical constraints determining built space - the provision of shelter and comfort - it is above all the psychological and emotional factors that should provide scope for our individual and social lives. The ability to experience our own world is a prerequisite to thinking of others and entering into a mutual relationship with the community.*

Habitation means occupying a space and imbuing it with life in one's own individual way: finding one's personal form of expression, communicating it to others, and experiencing a sense of freedom and security within "one's own four walls" and as a result of these walls. Somewhere deep inside us, imprinted in our psyche, are tribal memories of primal spaces, images we share with many other people. But there are also spaces in our consciousness, tinged with personal experience, that can spark off individual feelings and associations.

Changes in the economic and social communities to which a person belongs result in changes in his forms of work and habitation. This calls for flexible structures that will permit the individual to organize his life in accordance with his own requirements for privacy and community. Active participation in the individual design of this realm, more scope for personal development and co-determination all help to create a stronger sense of identification and neighbourliness. Buildings of greater depth, different storey heights and room sizes, and unfinished spaces allow greater freedom of choice and personal latitude for design. ◻ ◻ ◻

1.

1. Die fließenden Räume ermöglichen individuelle Grenzbeziehungen. ■ *Spaces flow into each other, enabling individual boundaries to be drawn and relationships to be established across them.*

2. Erholungsbereiche im Park am See und im Café und „Abenteuerspielplätze" für junge Bürger und Künstler. ■ *Recreation areas in the park, by the lake and in the café; "adventure playgrounds" for young people and artists.*

3. Innen und außen – Verbindung mit der Natur. ■ *Indoors and outdoors - links with nature.*

4. Plätze an den Grenzen zwischen Architektur und Natur laden ein zu Besinnung und Reflexion. ■ *Situations on the borders between architecture and nature invite visitors to pause and reflect.*

5. Identifikation durch unterschiedliche Häuser, Außenräume und Wohnzonen. ■ *Different house types, external spaces and living zones help to create a sense of identification.*

6. Verschiedene Raumgrößen und -qualifikationen im Bürohaus. ■ *Rooms of various sizes and for different purposes in the office tract.*

2.
3.

4.
5.
6.

Wohnhaus in der Josephstraße, Köln ■ *House in Josephstrasse, Cologne*

1. 2.
Alle Räume haben Beziehung zum Grün durch die üppig berankte Fassade und die vielen Terrassen und Dachgärten. ■ *All rooms are related to green, landscaped outdoor spaces in the form of the luxuriant vegetation climbing up the façade and the many terraced areas and roof gardens.*

Ein Stadthaus in Köln – in einer gesichtslosen Straße aus der Nachkriegszeit – beherbergt eine große Familie und ein Büro mit den unterschiedlichsten Bedürfnissen und Wünschen. Auf 13 versetzten Ebenen entstehen Räume mit differenzierten Qualitäten vom Hobbyraum mit Patio zur Straße über das Büro am Innenhof bishin zum zentralen Herd des Hauses und den individuellen „äußeren" Räumen in den oberen Randbereichen. Verschiedene Stufen von Privatheit und Öffentlichkeit treten in Beziehung, sei es nach außen zum Straßenraum als auch nach innen zur Mitte des Hauses. Eine zu öffnende Klappe in der Decke erweitert den zentralen Raum je nach jahreszeitlichen Bedürfnissen von Rückzug oder Ausdehnung. Im geschlossenen Zustand gibt es ein „Kindergeschoß".
Alle Räume haben Beziehung zum Grün durch die üppig berankte Fassade und die vielen Terrassen und Dachgärten. Die hohe Ausnutzung des Grundstücks durch die große Gebäudetiefe ist wirtschaftlich und ökologisch sinnvoll. Durch die großzügige Verglasung und innere Fenster werden auch dunklere Zonen belichtet.

Herausforderung für die Straße
Die Berücksichtigung des Ortes muß Provokation sein, wenn, wie in diesem Falle, die Nachbarschaft - wiederaufgebaute Häuser mit Lochfassaden - schwach ist. Verstöße gegen die Bauordnung, wie hier die beiden weit auskragenden Erker, sind dann angemessen, wenn eine neue Qualität erreicht werden soll.

Wohnen in der Stadt
Eine hohe, in diesem Falle 4-fache Ausnutzung des Bodens ist kein Verstoß, sondern eine soziale Verpflichtung. Es werden vorhandene Einrichtungen der Stadt optimal genutzt, der Zersiedelung entgegengewirkt und Kommunikation gefördert. Dafür müssen zusätzliche Angebote gemacht werden, die das Leben in den versteinerten Städten verbessern: bei diesem Stadthaus für eine große Familie bestehen diese Angebote aus Räumen für einen Laden oder eine Kindergruppe, aus Übergangszonen wie der kleinen Spielecke am Hauseingang, aus Erkern, die das Leben auf der Straße mit dem im Hause verbinden etc.

Licht und Transparenz
Die totale Befensterung und große Haustiefe gibt den Bewohnern Wahlfreiheit. Ein Nebenprodukt der facettenartigen Befensterung ist reflektierende Sonne. Die versetzten Geschosse ergeben innere Fenster und dadurch großzügige Durchblicke und sonnige Nordzimmer.
Große Klappen mit Flaschenzügen ermöglichen eine vertikale Veränderung der Räume, wodurch große Sommerräume mit Galerien oder kleine Winterhöhlen gebildet werden können. □ □ □

2.

1.

A town house in a somewhat faceless, post-war street in Cologne has been designed to accommodate the extremely diverse needs and wishes of a large family and an office. Scattered over 13 different levels are rooms of quite different qualities, from a workroom with a patio facing on to the street or an office with an aspect to an internal courtyard, to the central "hearth" of the house and the individual external spaces in the upper peripheral zones of the building. Various degrees of privacy exist, from seclusion to openness, and these enter into different relationships with each other - outwardly, for example, to the public street space, or inwardly to the heart of the house.

An openable flap in the ceiling of the central space allows it to be extended or closed off, depending on the season and whether one wishes to retire or communicate with other realms. When the flap is closed, the upper level can be used as an additional children's area. All rooms have a relationship with green, landscaped outdoor spaces in the form of the planted façade and the many terraced areas and roof gardens. The intense exploitation of the site as a result of the great depth of the building makes sense both economically and ecologically. The broad areas of external glazing in conjunction with internal windows facilitate the lighting of inner zones that would otherwise be dark.

1. 2. 4. 5.
Verschiedene Stufen von Privatheit und Öffentlichkeit treten in Beziehung, sei es nach außen zum Straßenraum als auch nach innen zur Mitte des Hauses. ■ *Various degrees of spatial privacy and openness exist, and these enter into different relationships with each other - outwardly to the street and inwardly to the heart of the house.*

3. Eine Deckenklappe erweitert den zentralen Raum je nach jahreszeitlichen Bedürfnissen von Rückzug oder Ausdehnung. Im geschlossenen Zustand gibt es ein „Kindergeschoß". ■ *An openable flap in the ceiling of the central space allows it to be extended or closed off, depending on the season and whether one is in a retiring or an expansive mood. When the flap is closed an additional "children's floor" is created.*

7. Auf 13 versetzten Ebenen entstehen Räume mit differenzierten Qualitäten vom Hobbyraum mit Patio zur Straße, über das Büro am Innenhof, zum zentralen Herd des Hauses und den individuellen „äußeren" Räumen in den oberen Rändern. ■ *Scattered over 13 split levels are rooms of quite different qualities, from a workroom with a patio facing on to the street or an office with an aspect to an internal courtyard, to the central "hearth" of the house and the individual "outer" spaces in the upper peripheral zones of*

3.

A challenge for the street

In cases such as this, where the neighbouring buildings are examples of poor, post-war housing reconstruction - plain façades with openings punched in them - any attempt to respond to the location must take the form of a provocation. Infringements of building regulations, such as the two balcony/bay window structures cantilevered far out over the street, are only right and proper if one is to achieve a new urban quality in such a situation.

Living in cities

An intense exploitation of the site - in this case, a floor area four times the site area - is not an offence, but a social duty. Existing urban services are optimally used, a step is taken against urban sprawl, and social communication is stimulated. In return, additional facilities have to be provided to improve the quality of life in our cities of stone. In the case of this town house for a large family, these facilities take the form of space for a shop, a crèche or a children's play group, transitional zones such as the small play area in the entrance, and balconies and bay windows, all of which serve to create an interaction between the house and the street.

6. Die hohe Ausnutzung des Grundstücks durch die große Gebäudetiefe ist wirtschaftlich und ökologisch sinnvoll und durch die großzügige Verglasung sowie innere Fenster werden auch dunklere Zonen belichtet. ■ The intense exploitation of the site as a result of the great depth of the building makes sense both economically and ecologically. The broad areas of external glazing in conjunction with internal windows facilitate the lighting of inner zones that would otherwise be dark.

Light and transparency

The complete fenestration of the outer faces of the house and the great depth of the building allow the occupants a wide range of choices. A by-product of the facetted construction of the windows is the deflecting action they have in conjunction with the sun.

The setting-back of certain storeys, together with the provision of internal windows, results in long vistas through the building with sunny rooms even on the north face. Large opening flaps with tackle-blocks permit changes in the vertical form of certain rooms. In this way, generous summer spaces with gallery levels can be created, or small, snug dens for the winter. □ □ □

Kommunikation ■ *Communication*

Soziales Erleben als Grundbedingung unseres Seins kann als positive Erfahrung nur auf Freiwilligkeit beruhen. Die räumlich baulichen Anlagen, die Kontakte und Nachbarschaften entstehen lassen, finden in den Grenzbereichen von öffentlich und privat statt. Die Grenzen und Zwischenräume können Kommunikation entstehen lassen oder verhindern. Aus der Sicherheit des privaten Refugiums und der Wahlfreiheit zwischen Rückzug und Öffnung nach außen, kann sozialer Kontakt entstehen. Das Wohnumfeld schafft die Schwellenbereiche. Vorgärten und Terrassen als abgegrenzte Territorien, schon im öffentlichen Raum und doch noch „bei sich zu hause", Vorzonen vor den Eingängen, kleine „places" zum Verweilen, zum Sehen und Gesehenwerden, Balkone und Erker, die den Kontakt zur Straße und zum Platz herstellen; Treppenhäuser als kommunikative Räume, Eingangssituationen, die mehrere Funktionen zulassen, sind architektonische Elemente für mehr Kommunikation. Integration von Wohnen, Arbeiten, Bildung und Freizeit und kleinere soziale Netze mit mehr Verfügungsrechten über alle Funktionen des Lebens schaffen Urbanität im städtischen Kontext. ■

Social involvement as a prerequisite for our existence can be a positive experience only if it is voluntary. Built spatial forms that stimulate contacts between neighbours are to be found in the transitional zones between the public and private realms.

The boundaries and the intermediate spaces between the two can stimulate communication or hinder it. Social contact can develop from the feeling of security gained in the private retreat of the home and from the choice one has between withdrawal or outwardness. The threshold areas are a product of the dwelling environment. Front gardens or forecourts as demarcated zones that seem to belong to the public realm, yet are part of one's own home; approach areas before an entrance; small recesses or places where one may linger and see and be seen; balconies, oriels or bay windows that establish contact with the street and the public open space; staircases as spaces for communication; entrance situations that provide scope for a number of activities - all these architectural elements are conducive to improved communication. The integration of habitation, work, education and leisure, together with smaller social networks that allow greater self-determination in the various functions of life, is conducive to a greater quality of urbanity in our towns and cities.

□ □ □

1.

1. Eine Siedlung braucht Gemeinschaftseinrichtungen. ■ *A housing estate needs communal facilities.*

2. Eine lebendige Atmosphäre prägt den Charakter des Bürgerzentrums. ■ *The civic center is distinguished by its lively atmosphere.*

3. Keine langen Flure, sondern spannungsvolle Räume bilden kleine Plätze. ■ *Exciting spaces and small intermediate zones instead of long corridors.*

4. Das Café und das Foyer als Stätten der informellen Kommunikation, Ausstellungs- und Multifunktionsräume als offizielle Orte der Begegnung. ■ *The café and foyer function as places of informal communication; the exhibition hall and multi-purpose spaces as formal places of encounter.*

5. Innenwelt und Straßenraum nehmen im Erker, der sich weit in die Straße vorschiebt, Beziehung auf. ■ *Indoor realm and public space enter into a relationship with each other via the oriel window that projects out over the street.*

6. Direkte Verbindung von Entwicklung, Montage und Verwaltung. ■ *Direct links between development, assembly and administration areas.*

7. Die offene Halle mit dem Sheddach im Zentrum schafft vielfältige Blickbeziehungen. ■ *The open hall with the shed roof in the middle affords a wealth of visual links.*

2.

3.

4.

5.

6.

7.

Wohnbebauung Spargelacker, Hannover ■ *Spargelacker Housing Development, Hanover*

Auf einem Grundstück in Hannover, Stadtteil Bemerode, sind 308 öffentlich geförderte Wohnungen entstanden. Von der anfänglich vorgeschriebenen Blockrandbebauung wurde zugunsten einer offenen Bebauung abgesehen. Auf dem von einer Ringstraße gefaßten Gelände gruppieren sich 13 Einzelhäuser in lockerer Anordnung um zwei zentrale Höfe. Die Häuser werden über den halbgeschossig nach unten versetzten Gartenbereich miteinander verbunden. Die zentrale Erschließung der Gebäude erfolgt - die Orientierung erleichternd - von der Ringstraße bzw. von der das Gelände durchlaufenden Straße aus. Den Bereich zwischen den Häusern erschließen vorwiegend fußläufige Wege, die sich zu kleinen baumbestandenen Plätzen öffnen. Aus der Verflechtung dieser kleinen „Grünzüge" ensteht ein Netzpark, der den Nord-Süd-Grünzug und die beiden inneren Höfe verbindet.

Notwendige Ergänzungen der Wohnungen, wie Seniorenwohnungen, Gemeinschaftsräume, Jugendtreffs, Werkräume im Gartengeschoß der Häuser sind mit dem Freiraumangebot (Arena, Kinderspielgeräte, Autowaschplatz, Lindenplatz) verflochten. Ein kleiner Kiosk wird die bessere Gemeinschaftsstimmung fördern. ▫ ▫ ▫

1. Der differenzierte Außenraum bietet vielfältige informelle Angebote der Erholung und Begegnung. ■ *A wide range of outdoor spaces offers great scope for informal recreation and meeting people.*

2. Viele Gemeinschaftseinrichtungen in zwei Höfen und in den Häusern, von der KITA bis zur Ausländerberatung fördern die Kommunikation der Bewohner und nachbarschaftliche Beziehungen. ■ *The many communal facilities in the two courtyard areas and in the housing blocks - from children's day care to advice for foreign residents - stimulate neighbourly relations and communication between tenants.*

3. Lageplan ■ *Site plan*

The development comprises 308 publicly financed dwellings on a site in Bemerode, a district of Hanover. Initial requirements for a peripheral development taking up the lines of the street block were dropped in favour of an open form of construction.

Thirteen individual blocks have been erected in a loose arrangement on the site, which is enclosed by a circular access road. The housing is grouped around two main courtyard zones.

1. 2. 3.
Eingangszonen als Übergänge mit „places" angelegt. Die Terrassen der Erdgeschosse sind durch Niveauversprung geschützt. ■ *Entrance zones are designed as transitional "places" with a sense of identity. The ground floor patios are screened off by virtue of their elevated position.*

4. 5.
Spielplätze, Wege in den Höfen, Mietergärten, EG-Terrassen, Balkone mit großen Öffnungen als innere Loggien, Dachgärten als Lauben. ■ *Playground areas, courtyard paths, tenants' gardens, ground floor patios, balcony-loggias combined with large openings, roof gardens as sheltered retreats.*

4.

5.

1. Der Bouleplatz als Festplatz.
   The boule area as a place for social events.

2. Abwechslungsreiche und nach außen offene Raumform eines mit Spielplätzen, Begegnungsecken und Gemeinschaftsfunktionen wie Kiosk, Mutter- und -Kind, Secondhand, besetzten Innenhofes.

The heterogeneous, outwardly open spatial form of a courtyard, with playground areas, corners for informal encounters and communal facilities such as a kiosk and spaces in the garden storey for mothers and children, flea markets, etc.

1.

The blocks are linked to each other via garden areas half a storey-height below street level. Primary access to the blocks is from the ring road or from the route running through the centre of the site. This facilitates a sense of orientation. The areas between the blocks are reached largely via pedestrian paths, which widen at various points to form small, tree-lined spaces. By connecting up these secondary, green, planted routes, a park was created with a network of paths that link the north-south landscaped strip and the two enclosed courtyard areas.

The standard housing was complemented by further accommodation and facilities such as old people's dwellings, community rooms, meeting points for young people, and workrooms in the garden storey of the blocks. These are linked with open-air facilities such as the arena, the children's playground equipment, a car-wash area and a lime tree square. A small kiosk will also enhance the sense of community in the future. ☐ ☐ ☐

2.

1. Zwei Häuser, eine Treppe. ■ *Two blocks served by a single staircase.*

2. Zwei Ateliers für Künstler im „Torhaus". ■ *Two studios for artists in the "gatehouse".*

3. Viele Übergangszonen zu den Spielplätzen regen lebendige Nachbarschaftsbeziehungen an. ■ *The many transitional zones leading to the play areas stimulate active neighbourly relations.*

Gartengeschoß ■
Garden floor

Erdgeschoß/1.Obergeschoß ■
Ground floor/First floor

Dachgeschoß ■
Roof garden storey

3.

Moderne Techniken ■ *Modern technology*

Die Baumethoden müssen dem Stand der Technik angepaßt werden. Dies soll bei der Erstellung als auch beim Unterhalt der Gebäude Berücksichtigung finden. Elementiertes Bauen, Vorfabrikation und sinnvolle Automation, wie auch neuartige Regel- und Steuerungstechniken bei der Energieversorgung, der Einsatz neuer Materialien und Verbindungstechniken, die in anderen Produktionszweigen entwickelt werden, sowie Verfahrensweisen industrieller Fertigung können das Bauen rationeller und ökonomischer gestalten und damit einen Beitrag leisten zur Steigerung unserer ökologischen, sozialen und individuellen Lebensqualität. ■ *Building methods must be adapted to conform with the latest state of technology. This applies to both the construction and maintenance of buildings. Component building systems, prefabrication and automation where justified, as well as new automatic control systems in the field of energy supply, the use of new materials and jointing techniques developed in other areas of production, and industrial manufacturing processes can all help to make the construction of buildings more rational and economical, thus improving the ecological, social and individual quality of life.* ■ ▫ ▫ ▫

1.

1. Lichtlenkungssysteme belichten die Arbeitsplätze im tiefen Erdgeschoß und sparen Kunstlicht. ■ *Optical lighting systems illuminate the workplaces by deflecting light into the depths of the ground floor areas and thus reducing artificial lighting needs.*

2. Die große Halle wird von einem filigranen Tragwerk überspannt.. ■ *The large hall is covered by a finely articulated roof structure.*

3. Exponierte Stahltragwerke ermöglichen den stützfreien Konferenzraum mit minimiertem Aufwand an Stahl. ■ *The form of the exposed steel structure enabled the conference hall to be built without intermediate columns and with a minimum amount of steel.*

4. Der Bogenträger überspannt den unterirdischen Multifunktionsraum. ■ *The bowstring girder over the underground multi-purpose space.*

5. Der gläserne Erker als Abhangkonstruktion in Holz und Stahl. ■ *The transparent oriel window is a suspended structure in timber and steel.*

6. Vorfabrizierte Elemente. ■ *Prefabricated elements.*

7. Die Galerie ist von den Stahlträgern des Daches abgehängt. ■ *The gallery is suspended from the steel roof beams.*

2. 3. 4.

5. 6. 7.

Büros und Montagehalle, Köln ■ *Offices and Assembly Hall, Cologne*

Das Entwurfskonzept für den Gewerbebau der Firma Geyssel in Köln-Ossendorf orientiert sich an den Funktionen Entwicklung, Verwaltung und Fertigung von Sondermaschinen.

Die Montagehalle umfaßt eine eingeschossige, 6 m hohe Halle mit eingezogenen Galerien und Glasoberlicht. Ihr fügt sich seitlich flankierend ein dreigeschossiges Bürogebäude an. Auch im Gebäudeinneren wird der enge Bezug der Arbeits-und Funktionsbereiche durch Glasflächen mit direktem Sichtkontakt in allen Geschossen erlebbar.

Die Büronutzung beinhaltet große, stützenfreie, sowie kleine Büroeinheiten, Besprechungs- und Sozialräume.

Das Bauvorhaben wurde in zwei Abschnitten realisiert und berücksichtigt sowohl eine geplante Hallenerweiterung um weitere vier Achsen, als auch eine mögliche Aufstockung des Bürogebäudes bei entsprechenden Nutzerwünschen.

Die abschließende Westfassade als transparente Glasfassade in Alu-Pfosten-Riegelkonstruktion setzt sich im vorgelagerten Treppenhausturm fort und unterstützt durch seine Lichtdurchlässigkeit u.a. das umgesetzte Energiekonzept.

Der Einsatz von Lichtlenksystemen im Erdgeschoß, bestehend aus holografischen Elementen, speziell entwickelten Lichtlenkdecken in Zusammenhang mit einer tagesabhängigen Kunstlichtsteuerung, reduziert den Bedarf an konventioneller Energie und stellt damit insbesondere einen wertvollen Beitrag zur zukunftsorientierten Bauaufgabe dar.

Iso-Floc gedämmte Außen-und Innenwände, Sonnenkollektoren zur Warmwassererzeugung, Brauchwassersammeltank für die WC-Spülung und RCL als Unterbau für Pflaster und Bodenplatte in der Halle sind weitere Maßnahmen für eine positive Energiebilanz. □ □ □

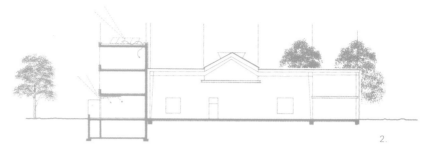

1. In einem polymorphen Gewerbegebiet ohne Bedingungen an formales Einfügen beschränkt sich das Gebäude auf die inneren Funktionen und den Akzent des Treppenturmes. ■ *In a heterogeneous industrial area with no points of reference for a formal integration of new developments, the building confines itself to an expression of the internal functions, with the staircase tower forming a salient feature.*

2. Schnitt ■ *Section*

3. Erdgeschoß ■ *Ground floor*

4. Obergeschoß ■ *Upper floor*

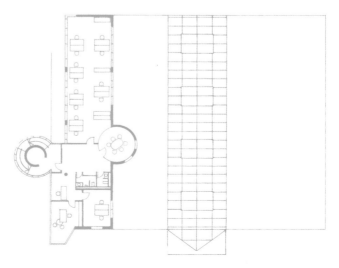

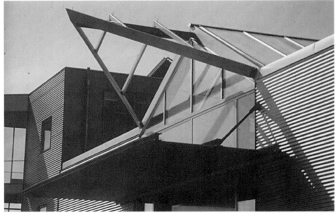

1.
2. 3.

The design concept underlying this industrial development for the Geyssel concern in Ossendorf, Cologne, reflects the three main functions of the complex: development, administration and the production of special-purpose machines.

The assembly tract comprises a single-storey, six-metre-high hall with galleries, and a glass lantern on the roof. Adjoining the hall on one side is a three-storey office block. Internally, the close relationship between production and other functional realms is reflected in the glazed areas that allow direct visual contact on all floors between the various departments.

The office tract comprises both large, continuous open areas and smaller office units, conference rooms and spaces for social purposes.

The development was realized in two stages and allows for a proposed extension of the hall by four additional bays, as well as a further storey on top of the office block should the need arise.

The design of the west façade - a transparent glass front in an aluminium post and rail construction - is continued in the projecting staircase tower. Its transparent, light-transmitting quality also supports the underlying energy concept.

5.

1. Die Treppe dreht weiter: für eine spätere Aufstockung des Büroflügels mit Wohnungen. ■ *The staircase continues its upward spiral for a further storey with dwellings, which may be added at a later date.*

2. 3. 4.
Die Halle ist für eine Erweiterung, das Bürogebäude für eine Aufstockung, z.B. mit Wohnungen vorgesehen. ■ *The hall can be extended, and an additional storey can be added to the office tract to provide space for dwellings, for example.*

5. Direkte Verbindung von Entwicklung, Montage und Verwaltung. ■ *Direct links between development, assembly and administration areas.*

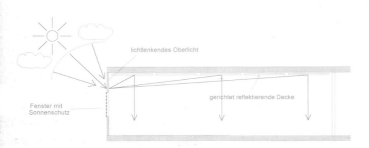

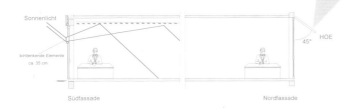

1. Reflektierende Lamellen in Verbindung mit Hologrammen in den Oberlichtverglasungen sparen Kunstlicht. ■ *Reflecting louvres in conjunction with holographic elements in the clerestory glazing strip reduce the amount of artificial lighting needed.*

On the ground floor, the use of optical lighting systems, consisting of holographic elements - specially developed light-directing soffits used in conjunction with daylight-related artificial light controls - reduces the consumption of conventional energy and thus represents a valuable contribution to future building design.

Other measures also help to achieve a positive balance of energy. These include Iso-Floc insulation to external and internal walls, solar collectors for heating water, a waste-water collection tank for flushing WCs, and recycled material as an underlayer for pavings and floor slabs in the hall.

□ □ □

3.

2. 4. „Industrielle" Materialien: Gußasphalt, Sichtbeton, MDF-Fensterbänke und Multiplexstufen. ■ *"Industrial" materials: mastic asphalt, exposed concrete, fibreboard window sills and laminated timber treads.*

3. Die runden, eingestellten Besprechungsräume schaffen Verbindung zwischen Montagehalle und Büros. ■ *The projecting circular conference spaces establish a link between the assembly shop and the offices.*

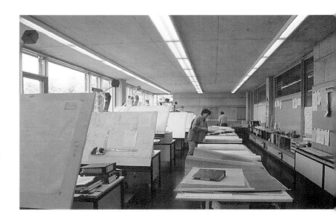

4.

Angemessene Mittel ■ *Appropriate means*

Soll der Einzelne über mehr Raum und Lebensqualität verfügen, muß wirtschaftlich günstig gebaut und finanziert werden. Die vorhandenen Ressourcen müssen besser ausgenutzt werden, so z.B. Baulandreserven in innerstädtischen Gebieten (Baulücken, Überbauungen). Sie sind angemessen zu verdichten und existierende Infrastrukturen vielfältiger und effizienter zu nutzen. Die Wiederverwendung von vorhandenen baulichen Strukturen und Materialien (Recycling), sinnvollere Baubetriebsformen und die Erbringung von Eigenbauleistung, Verwendung von Norm- und Serienprodukten sowie eine neue Definition von Standarts führen zu ökonomisch angemessenen Gebäuden. ■ *If the individual is to enjoy more space and increased living quality, we have to build more economically and find more efficient ways of financing construction. Existing resources have to be exploited more efficiently. This includes using reserves of inner-city land designated for building, infill schemes and building over existing transport routes, etc. Building densities should also be increased within reasonable limits, and existing infrastructures must be used more efficiently and for a greater range of purposes. The reuse (recycling) of building structures and materials, the implementation of rationalized forms of construction, the support of self-help initiatives, the use of standardized, serially made products and a new definition of standards would all contribute to a more relevant and economical form of building.* ▫ ▫ ▫

1. Dachaufsicht. ■ *View of roof.*

2. Kompaktes Gebäude, soweit die Bäume dies erlauben. ■ *A compact building form - as far as the trees permit.*

3. Eingegrabenes Gebäude mit wenig Abstrahlungsflächen. ■ *A compact structure sunk into the ground with few surfaces where energy is lost through radiation.*

4. Hohe Ausnutzung des Grundstücks auf 13 Ebenen. ■ *An intense exploitation of the site on 13 different levels.*

5. Zwei Häuser, eine Treppe. ■ *Two blocks served by a single staircase.*

6. Gußasphalt, Sichtbeton und MDF-Fensterbänke. ■ *Mastic asphalt, exposed concrete and fibreboard window sills.*

2. 3. 4.

5. 6.

Erweiterung des Bauturm, Köln ■ *Extension of Bauturm Offices, Cologne*

Im Zentrum Kölns, im Belgischen Viertel, ist in einer verdichteten Hinterhofsituation aus der Gründerzeit ein neuer Büroanbau entstanden. Zwischen zwei bestehende Wänden der Nachbargebäude wurden zwei Probebühnen des Bauturm-Theaters (Architekt: Marciniak + Pössl) und eine Halle für das Architekturbüro Schneider-Wessling eingefügt. Ein kleiner Hof mit einem Baum trennt die beiden Bereiche und schafft Bezug zum Außenraum.

Der neue Zwischenbau ist funktional und räumlich mit dem Altbau verbunden und über diesen erschlossen. Sechs Ebenen, halbgeschossig versetzt, schaffen eine kommunikative, offene Atmosphäre mit vielfältigen Blickbeziehungen. Das großzügige Sheddach belichtet das Zentrum der Halle. Glasböden unterstützen das Belichtungskonzept. Besprechungsräume, das Sekretariat und Büros liegen im Altbau und im neu gebauten Untergeschoß.

Das Untergeschoß ist in Stahlbeton gebaut, das Dach ist eine Stahlkonstruktion, von der die Galerieebene abgehängt ist. Die zwischen die bestehenden Wände gespannten Stahlträger sind mit Trapezblech gedeckt, mit Iso-Floc gedämmt und begrünt.

Die Fassade und das Sheddach ist eine Pfosten-Riegelkonstruktion aus Aluminium. Die Fußböden im Untergeschoß und Erdgeschoß sind in Anhydridestrich ausgeführt. Die Zwischenebene und Galerieebenen wurden als Stahlrahmen ausgeführt und mit Multiplexplatten bzw. Glasböden mit Punktraster belegt. Die Wände sind mit GK-Platten verkleidet und Iso-Floc gedämmt.

Mit der Überbauung erfolgte eine extensive und intensive Begrünung der Dachebenen; die überalterten Holunderbüsche wurden durch eine 10 m hohe Birke ersetzt. ■ ■ ■

1. Durch das großzügige Sheddach und die Glasböden dringt viel Licht in die Halle. ■ *The large shed roof and the glass floors allow a great deal of light to penetrate into the hall.*

2. Der kleine Hof mit der Birke und den Rankpflanzen schafft Beziehung zum Außenraum. ■ *The small courtyard with the birch tree and climbing plants establishes a link with the outdoor world.*

3. Der überdachte Hinterhof. ■ *The covered rear courtyard.*

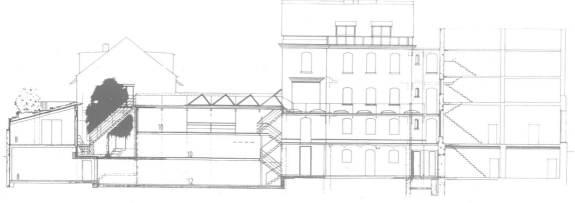

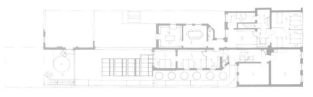

Dachgeschoß
■ *Plan of roof*

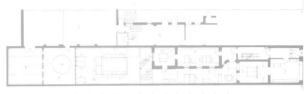

Eingangsebene
■ *Upper level*

Hofebene
■ *Lower level*

Untergeschoß
■ *Basement*

Grundrisse ■ Ground plans
1. Laden ■ Shop
2. Atelier ■ Studio
3. Besprechung ■ Conference room
4. Sekretariat ■ Secretarial office
5. Büro ■ Office
6. Foyer ■ Foyer
7. Theater ■ Theatre
8. Probebühne ■ Rehearsal stage
9. Hof ■ Courtyard
10. Halle ■ Hall
11. Café ■ **Café**
12. Archiv ■ Archives
13. WC ■ **WC**
14. Teeküche ■ Kitchenette
15. Technik ■ Mechanical services
16. Bibliothek ■ Library

In the densely developed "Belgian District" in the centre of Cologne, an office extension was inserted in the rear courtyard of a building dating from the end of the 19th century. Two rehearsal stages for the Bauturm Theatre (architects: Marciniak+Pössl) and a hall for Erich Schneider-Wessling's architectural practice were erected between the existing walls of the adjoining buildings. A small courtyard with a tree separates the two developments and creates a link with the outdoor world. Access to the new structure is via the existing building, to which it is also functionally and spatially connected.

The six split levels help to create a communicative, open atmosphere with a wealth of visual links. The large, glazed shed roof allows light to penetrate to the centre of the hall below. Internal conference rooms, secretarial and other offices in the existing building extend into the new basement level. The lighting concept is supported by the use of glass floors.

The basement construction is in reinforced concrete. The roof structure, from which the gallery is suspended, is in steel. Laid over steel beams spanning between the existing walls are trapezoidal-section ribbed sheets, insulated with Iso-Floc and covered with a planted layer.

1. 2. 3.

1. Die offene Halle mit dem Sheddach im Zentrum schafft vielfältige Blickbeziehungen. ■ The open hall with the shed roof over the middle gives rise to a wide range of visual links.

2. Die Galerie ist von der Stahlkonstruktion des Daches abgehängt. ■ The gallery is suspended from the steel roof structure.

3. Das Mitarbeiterteam. ■ Members of the team.

The façade and the glazed, lantern roof are in an aluminium post and beam form of construction. The basement and ground floors are sealed with anhydrite jointless screeds. The intermediate floor and the gallery levels consist of steel-framed laminated timber sheets and glass pavings with a spot-gridded surface. The walls are lined with gypsum plasterboard and insulated with Iso-Floc.

The courtyard development was complemented by an intensive planting of the roof surfaces. The aged elderberry bushes were replaced by a 10-metre-high birch tree.

Lebenslauf ■ *Curriculum vitae*

PROF. ERICH SCHNEIDER-WESSLING
ARCHITEKT BDA IM BAUTURM, KÖLN

Geboren 22.6.1931 in Wessling/Obb;
seit 1958 verheiratet, 5 Kinder
Studium an der TU München und in den USA bei
Frank. L. Wright.
Mitarbeit bei Richard J. Neutra, anschliessend
Projektleiter in Caracas / Venezuela
Architekturbüro in Köln seit 1960.

1968
Gründung des "BAUTURM" Köln; eine Gemeinschaft
von Architekten und Ingenieuren

Mitgliedschaft im Bund Deutscher Architekten
und im Deutschen Werkbund.

1969
Gründung der Arbeitsgruppe "Urbanes Wohnen",
zur Durchsetzung von Forderungen von
Betroffenen an das Wohnen in der Stadt.

1973
Lehrstuhl an der Akademie der Bildenden Künste
München und 1980/81 Gründung des
Aufbaustudiums "Reale Architektur".

1978
Gründung des Reichenauer-Architekturkreises
(Reale Architektur).

1984
Deutscher Städtebaupreis (Hesselbachpreis).
Wohnüberbauung Nikolaizentrum, Osnabrück

1985
The 1985 Richard Neutra Award for Professional Excellence.

1987
Fritz-Schumacher-Preis
für beispielhafte Leistungen auf dem Gebiete
der Architektur und des Städtebaus

1988
Gastprofessor am Massachusetts Institute of
Technology in Cambridge / USA.

1992
Architekturpreis der Westhyp-stiftung.
Projekt: Kommunikationszentrum; Leverkusen

1993
Auszeichnung Johann Wilhelm -Lehr Plakette
Projekt: Landeszentralbank Wiesbaden

1993
Architekturpreis Beton
Projekt: Kommunikationszentrum; Leverkusen

1995
Anerkennung Deutscher Architekturpreis
Projekt: Deutsche Bundesstiftung Umwelt, Osnabrück

PROF. ERICH SCHNEIDER-WESSLING
ARCHITECT BDA IN THE BAUTURM, COLOGNE

Born 22. 6. 1931 in Wessling, Upper Bavaria, Germany.
Married since 1958. Five children
Studied at the Technical University, Munich, and in the US
with Frank Lloyd Wright. Assistant with Richard J. Neutra;
subsequently project leader in Caracas, Venezuela
Own architectural practice in Cologne since 1960

1968
BAUTURM founded in Cologne, an association of
architects and engineers

Membership of the Association of German Architects (BDA)
and the German Werkbund

1969
"Urban Living" working group set up to service
the needs of the urban population and improve
the quality of life in cities

1973
Professor at the Academy of Visual Arts, Munich,
where the "Real Architecture" research course
was set up in 1980/81

1978
Reichenau Architectural Circle (Real Architecture)
founded

1984
German Urban Planning Prize (Hesselbach Prize).
Nikolai Centre housing development over
former street, Osnabrück

1985
The 1985 Richard Neutra Award for Professional Excellence

1987
Fritz-Schumacher-Prize
for exemplary achievement in the field
of architecture and urban Planning

1988
Visiting professor at Massachusetts Institute
of Technology, Cambridge, USA

1992
Architectural prize of the Westhyp Foundation.
Project: Communication Centre, Leverkusen

1993
Awarded the Johann Wilhelm Lehr Medal.
Project: Landeszentralbank Wiesbaden

1993
Architectural Prize for building in concrete.
Project: Communication Centre, Leverkusen

1995
German Prize for Architecture (acknowledgement).
Project: Federal German Foundation for the Environment,
Osnabrück

Werkverzeichnis ■ *Showcase*

Ausgeführte Projekte 1960 - 1970 ■ *Executed projects 1960 - 1970*
Wohnhaus M. Sepp, München
Wohnheim Familie Merzen, Remagen
Einfamilienhaus Familie Dopychai, Oberpleis
Sonderschule Köln-Holweide
Mehrfamilien- und Geschäftshaus Overkiwiz, Rösrath
Einfamilienhaus Familie Stockhausen, Kürten
Wohnhaus Familie Kemper, Wuppertal
Einfamilienhaus Gilka, Oberpleis
Zweifamilienhaus Familie Muthesius, Bonn-Holzlar
Haus Neven DuMont, Hoffnungsthal/Forsbach
Geschäftshaus Kolvenbach, Köln
Geschäftshaus Brendel, Köln
Einfamilienhaus Breith, Pirmasens
Einfamilienhaus Schulz, Forsbach
Gästehaus der Alexander von Humboldt-Stiftung, Bonn
Mehrfamilienhaus Rheinbay, Koblenz
Wohnhaus in Oberpleis
Mehrfamilienhaus Heger, Köln
Sanierung Wohnanlage Stift, Bad Godesberg
Umbau Cohnenhof, Köln
Einfamilienhaus Fittinghof, Hoffnungstal/Forsbach
Einfamilienhaus Zacharias, München
Musikhochschule Köln, mit Werkgruppe 7 im Bauturm
Neubau Galerie und Wohnhaus Rudolf Zwirner, Köln
Einfamilienhaus Löw, Forsbach
Einfamilienhaus von der Hude, Bonn-Holzlar
Überbauung Westbahnhof, Köln
Wissenschaftszentrum Ahrstraße, Bonn, mit Hautz / v. Dorp
Doppelwohnhaus Familien Hirsch und Heisenberg, Bonn
Gesamtschule, Rodenkirchen, Köln, mit Werkgruppe 7 im Bauturm

Wettbewerbe 1960 - 1970 ■ *Competitions 1960 - 1970*
Neubau Rathaus, Düsseldorf
Römisch-Germanisches Museum Köln, Köln
Gästehaus der Alexander von Humboldt-Stifung, Bonn
Montessori-Zentrum, Köln
Weltausstellung Montreal
Bezirkshallenbad Köln
Bahn-Überbauung München
Stadionbauten Olympiade 1972, München
Gymnasium Germering, Germering
Universität Trier
Wohnbebauung Römerlager, Bonn
Dienstleistungszentrum in Langenberg
Neubau Gemeindezentrum, Kreuzkirchengemeinde Bonn
Modellschule Weidenau mit Smrha

Ausgeführte Projekte 1971 - 1980 ■ *Executed projects 1971 - 1980*
Einfamilienhaus Jung, Aachen
Einfamilienhaus Möhler, Bonn
Mehrzweckhalle Waldbröhl, Waldbröhl
Einfamilienhaus Herrschmann, Kochel
Umbau Einfamilienhaus Schäfer, Köln
Einfamilienhaus Peddinghaus, Wuppertal
Wohnungsbebauung Bonn
Zweifamilienhaus von Dohnanyi, Bonn
Deutsche Schule, Teheran, mit Zeki Dinekli Bauturm
Wohnhaus Schneider-Wessling, Köln
Einfamilienhaus Horrig, Rheydt
Wohnhaus Wirsing, Leverkusen
Bebauungsplan Unterhaching mit Georg Penker, Ilse Walter
Haus Schoeller, Aachen
Werkdienstwohnungen Gesamthochschule, Siegen
Einfamilienhaus Kehr, Weilerswist - Metternich
Turnhalle für Modellschule Weidenau
Gesamthochschule Siegen, mit SI-Planer
Umbau Kommunikationszentrum, Osnabrück
Gesamtschule Bonn-Beuel, Bonn, mit Bauturm
Gesamthochschule Siegen: Allgem. Verf. Zentrale, Chemikalienlager, Hörsaal
Sanierungsplan Belgisches Viertel, Köln, mit Gruppe 49
Maschinenbauhallen Gesamthochschule, Siegen mit SI-Planer
Wohnbebauung Hardtberg, Bonn mit Steidle + Partner
Wohnhaus Petersen, St. Tropez
Bundesgartenschau Berlin, mit Georg Penker
Nikolai-Centrum, Osnabrück
Umbau Brügelmann-Haus, Köln, mit Gisbert Brovot
Raiffeisenkasse, Weßling mit Manfred Schneider
Einfamilienhaus Langen, Bad Homburg
Umbau Haus Stockhausen, Kürten

Wettbewerbe 1971 - 1980 ■ *Competitions 1971 - 1980*
Bebauung Gelände Loe-Kaserne, Bonn
Fußballstadion Köln
Bebauung Sanierungsgebiet Bonn - Bad Godesberg
Stadtkern Steinheim
Altenzentrum Spenge mit Bauturm
Bundesbauten Bonn mit Bauturm
Parkhaus Osnabrück
Bürohaus Würzburg
Schulzentrum Viersen
Bundeswehrverwaltungszentrum, München, mit Arlt, Philipp + Partner
Ortsstudie Losheim, mit Gellenberg;
Städtebaulicher Wettbewerb Wachtberg/Ortsteil Berkum
Platzgestaltung Ledenhof, Osnabrück
Bürgerhaus Troisdorf
Uni Passau
Pressehaus Kölner Stadtanzeiger, Köln
Kurmittelzentrum Aachen
Kreishaus, Köln
Rathaus Viersen mit Busmann + Haberer;
Internationales Begegnungszentrum, München
Bürgerzentrum Hürth, mit Busmann + Haberer
Gutachten Brückenstraße Köln
Freizeitzentrum Kemnade, mit Georg Penker, Otto Steidle
Städtebaulicher Vorentwurf Gerresheim-Torfbruch, Düsseldorf, mit Penker, Steidle, Spieker, Zlonicky
Gemeindezentrum Weßling
Wettbewerb Solartypologie Melkerei Landstuhl
Wettbewerb Bundesgartenschau Düsseldorf, mit Georg Penker
Wettbewerb Lützowstraße Berlin "Stadthäuser"
Wettbewerb Landeszentralbank, Köln
Sanierung Stollwerck-Gelände, Köln

Ausgeführte Projekte 1981 - 1990 ■ *Executed projects 1981 - 1990*
Mehrfamilienhaus Brinkmann, Köln
Gestaltung Rheingarten, Köln, mit mit Georg Penker
Landeszentralbank, Wiesbaden
Umbau Einfamilienhaus Behring / Müller, Bonn
Einfamilien-Solarhaus Mentzel, Landstuhl
Umbau Kartonagenfabrik zu Galerie- und Atelierhaus, Köln

Werkverzeichnis ■ *Showcase*

Einfamilienhaus Vahle, Köln
Rheingarten Pavillon, Köln
Einfamilienhaus Bornheim, Bornheim
Einfamilienhaus Jens, Esslingen
Einfamilien- Solarhaus Jähn, Zweibrücken
Solarhaus Familie Swietlik, Einöd
Solarhaus Stoll, Saarbrücken
Umbau Hinterhaus Aachener Str. 24, Köln
Doppelhaus Familien Hofferberth und Koch, Kronsberg
Mehrfamilienhaus am Lützowufer, Berlin
Einfamilienhaus Ruegger, Neerach/Schweiz
Einfamilienhaus Schatt, Busenberg, mit Claus Steffan
Umbau Galerie + Atelierhaus Zwirner, Köln
Bahnhofsvorplatz Osnabrück
Verkehrsberuhigung Rövekamp, Harsewinkel
Mehrfamilienhaus Kimmerle, Metzingen
Einfamilienhaus Schoop, Baden/Schweiz, mit Teaching Office, München
Einfamilienhaus Gäble, Poing, mit Claus Steffan

Wettbewerbe 1981 - 1990 ■ *Competitions 1981 - 1990*
Gutachten Energiemuseum, Hamm
Wettbewerb Rheingarten, Köln, mit Georg Penker
Wohnungen in Wetter
Gutachten Bundesgartenschau , Berlin, mit Georg Penker
Neubau Landeszentralbank, Mainz
Wettbewerb Josef-Haubrich-Hof, Köln, mit Gisbert Brovot
Deutsche Botschaft, Helsinki
Verwaltungsgebäude Goethe-Institut, München
Gutachten Heumarkt, Köln, mit mit Gisbert Brovot
Domhof, Osnabrück
Städtebl. Ideenwettbewerb Lennep, Remscheid
Postgebäude, Bonn
Vitihof Tiefgarage, Osnabrück
Bebauung Türkenkaserne München
Erweiterung Virchow-Klinikum, Berlin
Arbeitsamt, Dortmund
Erweiterung Sparkasse Hannover
Verwaltungsgebäude Deutsches Reisebüro, Frankfurt
Wohnbebauung Rauchgründe, Salzburg mit Teaching Office, München
Gutachten Märkisches Viertel, Berlin
Stadthalle Remscheid
Documenta-Halle, Kassel, mit Teaching Office, München
Hohwaldstrasse Frankfurt, mit Teaching Office, München
Städtebaulicher Ideenwettbewerb Altenerding Süd, Erding, mit Teaching Office, München
Projektstudie City Bergkamen, mit Teaching Office, München
Schokoladenmuseum Köln
Kammerspiele München, mit Teaching Office, München
Rathaus Nippes, Köln
Wettbewerb Sittarder Straße, Aachen

Ausgeführte Projekte und Projekte in Ausführung 1991 - 1995
■ *Executed projects and projects in preparation 1991 - 1995*
Bürogebäude der „Selbsthilfe" Rentenkasse d. Deutschen Caritas, Köln
Kommunikationszentrum der Bayer AG, Leverkusen
Rathaus und Bürgerhaus, Kaarst
Geschäftszentrum in Kaarst
Büros-und Montagehalle Firma Geyssel, Köln-Ossendorf
Wohnungsbau am Spargelacker, Hannover,
mit Büro Muth + v.d. Lage und Büro Raumplan 3, Argyrakis (GBH)
Erweiterung des Bauturm Köln, Köln
Verwaltungsgebäude Deutsche Bundesstiftung Umwelt, Osnabrück
Mehrfamilienhaus Bismarckstrasse, Köln
Musikschul- und Bürogebäude Media Park, Köln
Kaiser-Karl-Klinik, Bonn,
Wohn u. Geschäftshaus Grubenstrasse, Rostock
Prof. Georg-Lenz-Klinik, Masserberg
Ökologisches Mehrfamilienhaus, Köln
Pavillon des Hauptgesundheitsamtes, Bremen
Akademie und Gästehaus Guxmühlen, Nümbrecht

Wettbewerbe 1991 - 1995 ■ *Competitions 1991 - 1995*
Technologiezentrum Oberhausen, mit Teaching Office, München
Rahmenplanung Breslauer Platz Köln, mit Bauturm Busmann + Haberer
Realisierungswettbewerb Deutschherrenufer, Frankfurt a.M., mit Karl Sorge
Wettbewerb Umweltbehörde, Hamburg, mit Claus Steffan
Städtebaulicher Ideen-und Realisierungswettbewerb Rosenstein, Stuttgart
Kindergarten St. Josef, Merzig, mit Teaching Office, München
Wettbewerb Französisches Viertel, Tübingen, mit Ilse Walter
Rheinauhafen, Köln, mit Busmann+Haberer
Weltausstellung EXPO 2000, Hannover, mit Claus Steffan, Georg Penker, Tom Sieverts, Ulrich Gerlach, Frei Otto
Wohnbebauung Düsseldorf-Gerresheim, Düsseldorf, mit Ilse Walter
Stadthalle und Hotel Lemgo, mit Teaching Office, München
Stadtsanierung Greifswald, mit Teaching Office, München
Wettbewerb Breslauer Platz, Köln
Gelände der Krupp AG Essen
Wettbewerb Dresden - Kalitz, Rathaus Dresden
Wohnbebauung Schlossstraße Salzburg, mit Teaching Office, München
Wettbewerb Spreebogen, Berlin
Erweiterung Musikschule in Detmold
Neubau Verwaltungsgebäude Norddeutsche Metall-Berufsgenossenschaft, Hannover
Wohnbebauung Behringstraße, Hamburg, mit Claus Steffan
Nahversorgungszentrum Prosper III, Gelsenkirchen, mit Karl Sorge
Gewerbepark Lipperfeld, Oberhausen, mit Claus Steffan
Wettbewerb Georg-Brauchle-Ring, München, mit Claus Steffan
Ökologische Stadtentwicklung Süssenbrunn, Wien
Städtebaulicher Ideenwettbewerb Kronsberg, Hannover,
mit Claus Steffan, Ulrich Gerlach
Informationszentrum Blumberger Mühle Schorfheide
Gutachten "Maxtorhof", Nürnberg
Wohnen in Kleinmachnow, Berlin
Städtebaulicher Ideenwettbewerb Bad Honnef
Landeszentralbank Sachsen-Anhalt, Halberstadt
Wettbewerb Graf Bismarck, Gelsenkirchen, mit Claus Steffan;
Städtebaulicher Wettbewerb Gutenbergstraße, Kiel, mit Claus Steffan;
Wohnbebauung Heide-Süd, Halle, Kooperatives Verfahren mit
Büro Trajan und Büro Graul;
Gutachterverfahren Wohnen am Neuen Garten, Potsdam
Therapiezentrum Bad Saarow-Pieskow
Gutachterverfahren Wohnungsbau Berlin Marzahn-Nord, mit Heinz Neußl
Städtebaulicher Ideenwettbewerb "Wolbeck-Nord", Münster
Realisierungswettbewerb Neubau eines kirchlichen Verwaltungsgebäudes, Dresden
Verwaltungsneubau Industrie-und Handelskammer, Karlsruhe,
mit Claus Steffan

Werkverzeichnis, Mitarbeiter ■ *Showcase, Staff*

Die sieben im Katalog vorgestellten Projekte ■ ***The seven projects published in this catalogue***

Neue Stadtmitte Kaarst ■ ***New Civic Centre, Kaarst***
Rathaus und Bürgerhaus ■ *Town hall*
Hanno Lagemann, Pablo Molestina, Barbara Schaeffer, Dirk Scherdin. Statik: ■ *Structural engineering:* Konstruktionsgruppe für Bauwesen, Köln, HSLE: ■ *Mechanical services:* HL-Technik, Düsseldorf, Lichtplanung: ■ *Lighting planning:* Dinnebier, Wuppertal, Bauphysik: ■ *Construction physics:* Büro Trümper + Overath, Bergisch-Gladbach,
Geschäftszentrum ■ ***Business centre***
Thomas Nebel, Karsten Unkhoff, Deborah Ascher Barnstone, Reinulf Padberg, Carsten Niemeyer, Margret Lorch-Schneide, Landschaftsplanung: ■ *Landscape planning:* Bödecker, Wagenfeld +Partner, Düsseldorf, Statik: ■ *Structural engineering:* Büro A W D, Köln, HSLE: ■ *Mechanical services:* IFTG Böllecke, Köln, Bauphysik: ■ *Construction physics:* Büro Graner, Bergisch-Gladbach, Planungsbeginn: 1988, Fertigstellung: 1995
■ *Planning start: 1988, completion: 1995*

Deutsche Bundesstiftung Umwelt, Osnabrück ■ ***Federal German Foundation for the Environment, Osnabrück***
Kai Holthöwer, Dr. Mathias Höhne, Ulrich Klein, Katja Sann, Reinulf Padberg, Martin Rudolf (Landschaftsplanung ■ *Landscape planning*), Statik: ■ *Structural engineering:* Konstruktionsgruppe für Bauwesen, Köln, Bauphysik: ■ *Construction physics:* Büro Graner, Bergisch-Gladbach, HSLE: ■ *Mechanical services:* HL-Technik, München, Fassade: ■ *Façades:* Büro Schiller, Kornwestheim
Planungsbeginn: 1991 Fertigstellung: 1995
■ *Planning start: 1981, completion: 1995*

Kommunikationszentrum der Bayer AG, Leverkusen ■ ***Bayer AG Communication Centre, Leverkusen***
Ilse Walter, Andres Micnucci, Burkhart Richter, Holger Weber, Angela Schneider, Dirk Scherdin, Statik: ■ *Structural engineering:* Büro Hauschild, Leverkusen, HSLE: ■ *Mechanical services:* KSP, Köln, Bauphysik: ■ *Construction physics:* Büro Overath + Trümper, Bergisch-Gladbach, Landschaftsplanung: ■ *Landscape planning:* Georg Penker, Neuss, Lichtplanung: ■ *Lighting planning:* Büro Dinnebier, Wuppertal
Planungsbeginn: 1988, Fertigstellung: 1991
■ *Planning start: 1988, completion: 1991*

Wohnhaus in der Josefstraße, Köln ■ ***House in Josephstrasse, Cologne***
Fred Bohl, Statik: ■ *Structural engineering:* Gerhard Tripler, Köln
Planungsbeginn: 1970, Fertigstellung: 1974
■ *Planning start: 1970 completion: 1974*

Wohnungsbau am Spargelacker, Hannover
■ ***Spargelacker Housing Development, Hanover***
Prof. Erich Schneider-Wessling (Haus Nr. 14, 18, 20, 30, 32) Andreas Hopp, Ralf Extra, Martin Rudolf, Ines Bongard-Deeters, Cornelia Jung, Uwe Trübenbach, Carsten Bruns, Statik: ■ *Structural engineering:* Konstruktionsgruppe für Bauwesen, Köln, HSLE: ■ *Mechanical services:* IFTG Faxel und Böllecke, Köln, Müllkonzept: ■ *Waste disposal concept:* Frau Brinkmann-Herz, Köln, Wohnberatung: ■ *Housing advisory service:* empirica, Bonn
mit:
Büro Muth + v. d. Lage, Hannover (Haus Nr. 8, 12, 22, 24),
Büro Raumplan 3, Kellner, Schleich, Wunderling, Hannover (Haus Nr. 26, 28, 34)
Dipl.-Ing. Argyrakis, GEH, Hannover (Haus Nr. 10, 16)
Planungsbeginn: 1991, Fertigstellung: 1995
■ *Planning start: 1991 completion: 1995*

Büros-und Montagehalle Firma Geyssel, Köln ■ ***Offices and Assambly Hall, Cologne***
Michael Krumbe, Gabriela Decker, Dirk Scherdin, Statik: ■ *Structural engineering:* Konstruktionsgruppe für Bauwesen, Köln, HSLE: ■ *Mechanical services:* Büro INCO, Aachen, Lichtplanung: ■ *Lighting planning:* Prof. Müller, ILB, Köln
Planungsbeginn: 1991, Fertigstellung: 1994
■ *Planning start: 1991, completion: 1994*

Erweiterung des Bauturm, Köln ■ ***Extension of Bauturm Offices, Cologne***
Dorothee Schneider, Tobias Kröll, Edgar Haupt, Andrea Denzer, Statik:
■ *Structural engineering:* Konstruktionsgruppe für Bauwesen, Köln, Bauphysik:
■ *Construction physics:* Büro Graner, Bergisch-Gladbach
Planungsbeginn: 1991, Fertigstellung: 1994
■ *Planning start: 1991, completion: 1994*

Mitarbeiter im Büro seit 1960 in alphabetischer Reihenfolge:

Carlos Albuquerque, Eckhard Alfes, Deborah Ascher-Barnstone, Bernd Ax, Antje Bandau, Heidi Bartram, Hans Georg Baum, Michael Behr, Hagen Beinhauer, Sigrid Blankenburg, Alfred Bohl, Ines Bongard-Deeters, Anni Borrell, Susanne Brachthäuser-Berg, Jutta Bräuer-Mohry, Helmut Brinkhaus, Carsten Bruns, Alexia Chatzipetros, Gabriela Decker, Sabine Delhaes, Andrea Denzer, Verena Dietrich, Zeki Dinekli, Annemarie Dornheck Busscher, Ulli Driever-Demissie, Krafft-Aretin Eggert, Peter Elkin, Jürgen Engel, Ralf Extra, Ursula Feldmann, Jo Franzke, Hermann Freund, Ines Gross, Michael Güldenberg, Ingo Haas, Arthur Hachenberg, Heiner Hachenberg, Elham Hamdirad, Christoph Harings, Edgar Haupt, Dr. Mathias Höhne, Kai Holthöwer, Andreas Hopp, Octavianne Hornstein, Corinna Huboi, Martin Janda, Cornelia Jung, Dr. Hartmut Kahmen, Irfan Kandirali, Kazuhisa Kawamura, Alfred Keller, Ralf Kirchhoff, Ulrich Klein, Olaf Klöters, Eckhard Kluth, Peter Köhne, Michael Kraus, Tobias Kröll, Michael Krumbe, Per Krusche, Hanno Lagemann, Renate Laser, Michael Lauer, Margret Lorch-Schneider, Renate Lilic, Ulrich Malisius, Dana Meyer, Irini Milona, Pablo Molestina, Christiane Monkenbusch, Thomas Nebel, Carsten Niemeyer, Rafaela Nordhaus, Carlos Olazabal, Jaqueline Oosterhagen, Jürgen Opitz, Reinulf Padberg, Manfred Pilz, Peter Recker, Rolf Reckort, Hannelore Requardt, Burkhard Richter, Karl-Heinz Rosenstein, Christoph Rothschuh, Jens Rottland, Martin Rudolf, Andrea Rumpf, Gabriele Ruoff, Katja Sann, Barbara Schaeffer, Wolfgang Schein, Brigitte Scheliga-Gauchel, Dirk Scherdin, Hanno Schimmel, Horst Schlösser, Oliver Schmidt-Hansen, Angela Schneider-Sedlaczek, Dorothee Schneider, Gabor Dervisha Schneider, Günther Schneider, Nils Schneider, Rosa Schramm, Heinz-Georg Schreiber, Mariola Schröder, Peter Schuh, Willi Schulte-Rudolphi, Jost Henner Schwedes, Siegfried Seidel, Andrea Stachelhaus, Barbara Taha, Uwe Trübenbach, Markus Uhlenhaupt-Oldorp, Karsten Unkhoff, Ilse Walter, Holger Weber, Stefan Werner, Jeremy Whitehurst, Heribert Wiesemann, Detlef Wilken, Therese Yserentant, Maris Zanke

Impressum ■ *Acknowledgements*

Konzeption ■ *Conception*
Octavianne Hornstein, Johannes Busmann

Englische Übersetzung ■ *English translation*
Peter Green

Fotografien ■ *Photography*
Bayer AG: 34
Gabriela Decker: 58(2,3)
ESW: 29(5), 35(5), 46
Helke Rodemeier: 13-15, 18-21, 25, 26(1,2), 29(4,6), 33, 35(2-4), 36, 37(2), 40-43, 47-49, 52, 53, 57, 58(1), 59-61, 65, 66
Martin Rudolf: 50, 51
Sibylle Sauvin: 29(3)
Desiree Schneider: 16, 17, 27(3,4)
Foto Strenger: 24, 26(5), 28(1)
Ilse Walter: 37(3,4)

Gestaltung ■ *Graphic design*
logos Wuppertal, Ralf Wimbert

Lithografie ■ *Lithography*
logos Wuppertal

Druck ■ *Printing*
RGA. Druck Remscheid

© Verlag Müller + Busmann, Wuppertal; Prof. Erich Schneider-Wessling
ISBN 3-928766-19-8